SHADOWS of AUSCHWITZ

SHADOWS of AUSCHWITZ

A Christian Response to the Holocaust

HARRY JAMES CARGAS

CROSSROAD • NEW YORK

1990

The Crossroad Publishing Company
370 Lexington Avenue, New York, NY 10017

Originally published as *A Christian Response to the Holocaust*
by Stonehenge Books, Denver, Colo.,
copyright © 1981 by Harry James Cargas.
This revised edition copyright © 1990 by Harry James Cargas

Printed in the United States of America

Library of Congress Cataloging-in-Publication Data

Cargas, Harry J.
     Shadows of Auschwitz / Harry James Cargas. —
  Rev. ed.
         p.   cm.
     Includes bibliographical references.
     ISBN 0-8245-1030-5
     1. Holocaust (Christian theology)   2. Holocaust, Jewish
  (1939–1945)   I. Title.
  BT93.C37   1990
  261.2'6 — dc20   89-27766
                                              CIP

Contents

Acknowledgments

It hardly suffices to put a few words on paper as a form of gratitude for ongoing assistance given me by a number of people. Yet how else . . . ?

Adam and Judy Aronson, my friends, have been so supportive, in so many ways, and for so extended a period, that truly without their help this book, and much else that I write, would never have been completed.

While doing research at Yad Vashem Holocaust Memorial Center in Jerusalem, I was enthusiastically assisted by Chana Abells and knowledgeably guided by one of the world's great Holocaust scholars, Dr. Livia Rothkirchen.

I must say that whatever is of merit in my work on the Holocaust has been profoundly influenced by the writing and friendship of Elie Wiesel. More than anyone, this man continues to be my teacher. No doubt I have not learned enough; I shall continue to strive. My obligations to Wiesel are great and unrepayable. He knows that I shall attempt to fulfill them, nevertheless.

Many people went into the making of this revised volume. I cannot refrain from public thanks for the friendship, encouragement, and leadership shown to me by Alice and Roy Eckhardt, Edward Flannery, Eva Fleischner, Nora Levin, Marcie and Franklin Littell, and John Roth.

Sandy Jafee helped me personally in an extraordinary way, and my manuscript preparation, so complicated in a work such as this, was heroically assisted by Margret Brown and Susan Perabo.

I am happily obligated to say a special thank you to Dr. Jakob Stern and Dr. Arnold Kerr, without whose constant support this revised edition might not have been possible.

Foreword

It has been said often, and it can never be said enough: The Event remains unique, unlike any other. Product of History, it transcends History. The burden of its horror weighing upon all aspects of the human experience, it goes beyond everything. Auschwitz: the ultimate mystery. Impossible to enter it from the outside. Whoever has not lived through it will never know, never understand it. Treblinka: kingdom of another world, symbol of total defeat. There, humankind finds itself condemned, robbed of all hopes, all illusions.

The few survivors themselves will confirm it: the Event defies all analogy; it can only be compared to itself. It defies understanding as well as language. No one can comprehend or describe it. To explain is to diminish it, to generalize is to mutilate it. The Holocaust demands interrogation and calls everything into question. Traditional ideas and acquired values, philosophical systems and social theories — all must be revised in the shadow of Birkenau. Novelists and politicians, poets and moralists, theologians and scholars — all feel compelled to examine their consciences with regard to the Holocaust. Not to do so would mean to live a lie.

Although essentially Jewish, the Event has universal significance. It calls out to all people, but, of course, in different ways.

We all want to know: how was it possible? The killers killed and the world was silent. . . . The killers were able to kill because the world was indifferent. The indifference of those days obliges us to take a stand today.

This is what Harry James Cargas does in his upsetting and disturbing work that will make readers, whatever their faith, reflect and weep.

A fervent and faithful Christian, the author expresses his anguish and sadness: it is impossible to detach the Final Solution from its Christian context. The murder of six million Jews is at the same time part of Jewish and Christian history. On all levels, the questions are disturbing. How does one explain that a Hitler or a Himmler were never excommunicated by the church? that Pope Pius XII never judged it necessary or essential to condemn Auschwitz or Majdanek? that the killers came from Christian families and had received a Christian education? and that many Catholic and Protestant dignitaries had supported the Nazis?

Certainly, here and there, courageous Christians faced danger and came to the aid of the Jews; we shall be eternally grateful to them. But they were few in number. They were the exceptions. As a general rule, the Jewish victims rarely found refuge. In Christian Poland, so hostile was the countryside that those who escaped from the ghettos often returned to them; they feared the Poles as much as the Germans. In Lithuania too. In the Ukraine. In Hungary. And yet in all of these occupied countries, there were resistance movements that had their heroes and martyrs. Only the Jews were victims of the Nazi invaders and of their victims as well.

How is one to understand, to explain, this Christianity bereft of charity and compassion? As a Jew, I have always been reluctant to explore the question. Let us thank Harry James Cargas for having done so. The things he says about his Christian brothers and sisters and friends will be painful to them; one hopes they will not turn away. Thanks to this book, they will learn what others have hidden from them for so long: that the love of God is whole only if expressed through the love of human beings.

ELIE WIESEL
Translated from the French by Ellen S. Fine

Introduction

A Post-Auschwitz Christian

To call myself a Roman Catholic is to describe my spiritual development incompletely. It is more honest for me to say at this time in my life that I am a post-Auschwitz Christian, in the wider context of Western Christianity. The Holocaust event requires my response precisely as a Christian. The Holocaust is, in my judgment, the greatest tragedy for Christians since the crucifixion. In the first instance, Jesus died; in the latter, Christianity may be said to have died. In the case of Christ, the Christian believes in a resurrection. Will there be, can there be, a resurrection for Christianity? That is the question that haunts me. Am I a part of a religious body that in fact is a fossil rather than a living entity? Can one be a Christian today, given the death camps that, in major part, were conceived, built, and operated by a people who called themselves Christians and some of whom — records prove, their own words prove, eyewitness accounts prove — took pride in this work?

The failure of Christianity in the mid-twentieth century is monumental. Is it fatal? I need to know. This seems to me to be the main question facing people who today call themselves Christian.

It is too easy to say of those who lived and persecuted *or remained "neutral"* in Germany, Poland, Russia, Austria, Czechoslovakia, Latvia, Hungary, Bulgaria, Greece, France, and other nations during the Nazi era that, although they regarded themselves as Christians, they really weren't. That's too smug an answer. One implication of such a response is that we who now look back and say that "they weren't really Christian" are eager to submit ourselves as authentic Christians. How can we be certain that when

1

the time comes for us to be heroic Christians (in theory, at least, the expression is redundant!) we will not collapse? All women and men are failures at their religion in some degree. But have we Christians, with our history of the persecution of Jews — with the Inquisition, the Crusades, pogroms, antiSemitism and the Holocaust — established a tradition of failure from which there is no escape?

The reasons for my own personal conversion from one Christian church to Roman Catholicism at age nineteen are not important. The act of commitment is decisive, however. I wished to share then, as I do now, in the many and great glories of that institution. I think it proper to say that I was obsessed with becoming as good a Christian as I could. Today it may be more accurate to say that I am obsessed with judging that original obsession. Was it valid or not? Am I a fool to be an active member of a church that proclaims love as its motivating energy when historically . . . ?

I let the question hang. I'm not even sure how to ask it. Others will perhaps rephrase it as they too search. It is one comfort to me that I do know an increasing number of Christians who are engaged in such an investigation. To ask the question by oneself isolates one so greatly that it may be spiritually perilous. Raised in a tradition of fear of an all-powerful God who can punish the blasphemous — and questioning the validity of Christianity will be seen by some as blasphemy — the question can be explored only at serious risk to one's spiritual health. However, some reflective Christians are at the point today in their spiritual development that it is blasphemous *not* to raise the question.

Silence, which can be holy, can also be sinful. Silence in the face of the Holocaust, I submit, is truly blasphemy. It is part of Christian teaching that God exists in every person. We dare not forget, then, that one million Jewish child-Gods were murdered by the Nazis and their collaborators in World War II. Five million other Jewish-Gods were slaughtered there also. And countless of non-Jewish-Gods were massacred as well: Gypsies, homosexuals, Jehovah's Witnesses, political dissidents, etc.

My passion with what I call the Christian Holocaust derives from the statistics cited above. Some Jews have been suspicious of my motives — I cannot blame them, given the history of Jewish-Christian encounters. Some Christians have been suspicious of my motives as well. Their suspicions are less understandable.

Through all of this, I have come to the conclusion that Albert Camus was profoundly correct when he said that "on this earth there are pestilences and there are victims, and it's up to us, so far as is possible, not to join forces with the pestilences." And Elie Wiesel was profoundly correct when he wrote that "he who is not among the victims is with the executioners." And Viktor Frankl was profoundly correct when he concluded that "we may learn that there are two races of men in this world, but only these two — the 'race' of the decent man and the 'race' of the indecent man."

Thus I must conclude that to identify myself as a Roman Christian, in the shadow of recent history, is inaccurate, incomplete, even misleading. Culturally, of course, I am that, but spiritually I put on the mantle of a post-Auschwitz Catholic. It is in this concept that all of my work — indeed my life — is now rooted.

Chapter 1

Centuries of Christian Persecution of the Jews

The massacre of Jews in the Second World War, and all that accompanied that prolonged, monstrous event, is the greatest Christian tragedy since the crucifixion of Jesus. The Holocaust was the culmination, in great part, of Christian teachings about Jews, of misinterpreted and erroneous theology. After preaching love of others for nearly two thousand years it was, in the main, people who called themselves Christian who slaughtered women because they were Jewish, who slaughtered men because they were Jewish, who slaughtered babies because they were Jewish.

Jews have asked over and over again, Where was God at Auschwitz? — using the name of the most infamous of the death camps to stand for all of them. Some Jewish people of faith said that the torture and death of over five million Jews — more than one-third of all the Jews in the world — some said that these deaths, and the sufferings of the comparatively few who survived imprisonment, marked the birth pangs of the coming of the Messiah, that Messiah for whom the Jews have been waiting these many centuries. Other Jews were not so optimistic. One group, in a death camp, held a trial of God. They found God guilty of breaking the Covenant made with the chosen people and of abandoning them to the horrors of near annihilation.

Adolf Hitler, a baptized Catholic who was never excommunicated by Rome, implemented a policy of total destruction because, and only because, *he was able to*. Only because people willingly cooperated in individual and mass murders. Who, for example, were the lawyers and judges who supported and enforced antiSemitic laws? Who were the scientists who offered "proof" that Jews are inferior? Who were the medical personnel unconscionable enough to conduct torturous medical experiments? Who were the professors who ignored vicious lies in the texts they used, the journalists, authors, artists, film makers who participated in Nazi propaganda? Who were the Christian clergy who spread dishonest theology about Jews or kept silent while aware of atrocities? Who were the architects who designed the ovens into which people were delivered for cremation? Who meticulously executed the plans for the efficient gas chambers into which naked men, women, and children were herded to die? Who originated the design for the camps, those models of economical, technological destruction? Which firms bid on the contracts to build the camps, the gas chambers, the ovens? Who bribed whom to win the coveted contracts, to gain the chance to make a profit and serve the Führer by erecting houses of death and torture?

Who shaved the victims' heads, and all bodily hairs, to gain materials for cloth and rugs? We've heard of lampshades made from Jewish skins, of soap made from Jewish bodies, of "enforcers" throwing Jewish victims — most of them dead, but not all — into huge pits, of brutal guards crushing Jewish babies' skulls with rifle butts, and shooting aged and unhealthy Jews who couldn't keep up on forced marches, and forcing naked Jews to stand for hours in freezing weather for either convenience or amusement. Who were these tormentors? What of the train engineers who guided the cattle cars packed with starving, dying, dead Jews to their locales of internment? And what of the ordinary citizens of many European nations who, as the death trains passed through their communities, would throw bits of bread into the cattle cars to be entertained by watching famished Jews fight over the food in an agonizing display of attempt at survival?

Elie Wiesel provides an eyewitness account of just such an incident:

> In the wagon where the bread had fallen, a real battle had broken out. Men threw themselves on top of each other, stamping on each other, tearing at each other, biting each other. Wild beasts of prey, with

animal hatred in their eyes; an extraordinary vitality had seized them, sharpening their teeth and nails.

A crowd of workmen and curious spectators had collected along the train. They had probably never seen a train with such a cargo. Soon, nearly everywhere, pieces of bread were being dropped into the wagons. The audience stared at these skeletons of men, fighting one another to the death for a mouthful.

A piece fell into our wagon. I decided that I would not move. Anyway, I knew that I would never have the strength to fight with a dozen savage men! Not far away I noticed an old man dragging himself along on all fours. He was trying to disengage himself from the struggle. He held one hand to his heart. I thought at first he had received a blow in the chest. Then I understood; he had a bit of bread under his shirt. With remarkable speed he drew it out and put it to his mouth. His eyes gleamed; a smile, like a grimace, lit up his dead face. And was immediately extinguished. A shadow had just loomed up near him. The shadow threw itself upon him. Felled to the ground, stunned with blows, the old man cried:

"Meir. Meir, my boy! Don't you recognize me? I'm your father . . . you're hurting me . . . you're killing your father! I've got some bread . . . for you too . . . for you too . . . "

He collapsed. His fist was still clenched around a small piece. He tried to carry it to his mouth. But the other one threw himself upon him and snatched it. The old man again whispered something, let out a rattle, and *died amid the general indifference. His son searched him, took the bread, and began to devour it.* He was not able to get very far. Two men had seen and hurled themselves upon him. Others joined in. When they withdrew, next to me were two corpses side by side, the father and the son.

I was fifteen years old.[1]

So who were all the people who cooperated with Hitler's master plan? They were in the thousands, perhaps in the millions. How many people does it take to annihilate millions of human beings? How many more does it take to close their eyes to what's happening — to be neutral, lukewarm who will be spewed forth on Judgment Day according to their very own Christian tradition — in order to let the events continue?

One has only to think of the number of camps in order to begin to understand something of the magnitude of what went on. There were nearly 150 camps (for a listing see p. 128) where people

---

[1] *Night* (New York, 1960), pp. 102–103.

were forced into the loneliness of condemned existence. Yet even some Jews who survived were endangered when they returned after years of tortured living. Here is an account of a survivor who returned home to Poland after having endured the brutalities of several different camps in which she was imprisoned. I had asked how she and her husband, who has also been incarcerated, but in another camp, had been reunited.

After the war, in 1945, he was liberated in May. I was liberated on the 25th of April, by the Elba. We didn't know where to go. So we went home. Like everybody thinks, well, we'll go home, back to Poland. And we thought all of the people over there, the neighbors, will greet us with open arms. You know *we survived!* I was together with my sister and my mother, who had both been in camp with me. When we were liberated, we saw a long train going from Germany. We had nothing to lose so we jumped on the train because we were harassed from all sides — from the Russian soldiers, etc. So we jumped on a freight train which was going toward Poland. After a few days we arrived in our home town. You know how we looked from the concentration camp. But we had changed clothes.

At the edge of town we asked Polish people, "Are there any Jews here?" They said yes, there are a few back, but the minute they recognized us as Jews, "Why did you come back?" This is the first thing they said to us as Jews, "We thought that you are dead. Why did you come back?" But they did tell us where the few Jewish people were and we went there. The city hall in our town gave the Jews a few apartments in which to live — but concentrated in a few places. Here were a couple of Jewish families in one room. On another street there was a room with ten Jews. They were afraid to go out. When we came we found those families.

One Jewish lady said to us, come and live with me. I have two rooms and I'll give you one and I'll have one. We were lucky to get that apartment. It was like a garden apartment, three sides were apartments, the fourth used by the Russian military as their headquarters. This was in front of our apartment. We were lucky to be living behind them.

My husband, who thought as I did, came to the same place, and we were reunited. We lived there until September. I had been a dressmaker. I had learned something. It's not like here. Here you think about college. Over there we could only think about trades, to make a living. So when we came back a lot of Polish people brought me work to do.

One morning a lady runs into us: "My God, my God you are alive. I am so happy that you are alive." I said, "What's happened?" She was all shaken. She said to us, "Go away from here because they killed ten people in the apartment next to us — ten survivors." Ten survivors. They survived the concentration camps, killed by the Polish people. Ten people in one house. The attackers killed them with pistols and a machine gun. One of the murderers was from the militia, and he got a machine gun. We were lucky because the Russian militia was right in front of us, so we were not attacked. We didn't run away, we went to find out what happened.

We made a funeral for them. We all went to the cemetery with the Russian militia protecting us. *This was after the war in my home town.* We were afraid to go alone to the cemetery. A few weeks later we left our home town, then left Poland altogether. They found out who were the killers. A woman and two or three men. The woman was executed and I don't know what they did with the men.

The speaker's husband added this. "We were afraid because the hatred against Jews remained from before the war. We knew it would go on and on, the same thing. It was no use to be over there." When I asked the woman, later in our conversation, if she would wish ever to return to Poland, her answer was instantaneous "Never." Then she added, "Poland to me is blood."

Our Christianity

It is of the greatest import that we Christians know precisely how Jews react to us after persecutions, pogroms, Inquisition, ghettoization, Holocaust, tragic events that indicate major points of history in Jewish-Christian relations. Perhaps Eliezer Berkovits put it most succinctly when he insisted, as a Jew, that "all we want of Christians is that they keep their hands off us and our children!" That has to be an immensely painful statement for Christians to confront. Who, us? we will want to say. We who witness to the charity of Jesus Christ, the Lord and Savior of the world? It is supremely difficult for most of us to comprehend that we are seen as the persecutors, the torturers, the killers. But historically, that is how many Jews have perceived us.

It is enlightening to compare entries in the *Catholic Encyclopedia* and the *Encyclopedia Judaica*. The former has a relatively long entry on "Baptism." The latter has an article entitled "Baptism,

Forced." There is evidence that when Christianity came to be established as the dominant religion in the Roman Empire, many Jews were forcibly baptized, even though official church teaching was that baptism had to be accepted willingly. The practice was so common that in the fifteenth century Pope Martin V had to forbid categorically the baptism of Jewish children under twelve without their parents' permission. After this, certain Christians tried to circumvent the decree by going to supreme lengths to prove that what they did was the result of persuasion rather than force. In 1747, Pope Benedict XIV ruled that once baptized, even against the proscriptions of canon law, a child was to be considered Christian, regardless. This helped to swell the number of kidnappings of Jewish children by zealous Christians; the children, once baptized, were lost to their families.

That, then, gives a hint of how *we* are perceived by some others. One must say "we" because as Christians we are not just individuals but each is a member of a mystical body of faith that shares in certain glories and therefore shares in certain responsibilities as well. If it is *our* Christianity that gave the artistic and intellectual impetus to the period of history known as the Renaissance, then it is our Christianity that also sponsored the Inquisition. If it is *our* Christianity that saved learning through what some have labeled the Dark Ages, then it is *our* Christianity that also counseled expropriation of Jewish property in various countries in various centuries. Here, for example, are directives concerning Jews that are part of our Christian heritage:

First, their synagogue or school is to be set on fire and what won't burn is to be heaped over with dirt and dumped on, so that no one can see a stone or chunk of it forever.... Second, their houses are to be torn down and destroyed in the same way.... Third, they are to have all their prayerbooks and Talmudics taken from them.... Fourth, their rabbis are to be forbidden henceforth to teach, on penalty of life and limb.... On penalty of life and limb, they are to be forbidden publicly to praise God, to thank (God), to pray (to God), to teach (of God) among us and ours.... And furthermore, they shall be forbidden to utter the name of God in our hearing; no value shall be accorded the Jewish mouth (Maul) by us Christians, so that he may utter the name of God in our hearing, but whoever hears it from a Jew shall report him to the authorities or throw pig droppings on him.... Fifth, the Jews are to be deprived totally of walkway and streets.... Sixth, they are to be forbidden lending for interest and all the cash and holding of silver and gold are to be taken from them and put to one side for safe keeping.... Seventh, the young strong Jews and Jewesses are to have flail, axe and spade put into their hands.[2]

Do these sound like the words of some Nazi officer, caught up in the spirit of trying to rid the world of Jews? They are not. They form the teaching of Martin Luther some four centuries before the Holocaust.

There is no question that there is no collective Christian guilt over the sinful treatment of Jews over the ages. To be a true Christian is to believe in sin; to believe in sin is to know that what *some* Christians have done to *some* Jews, or have allowed to be done to some Jews, is sinful. For one not to recognize this is morally to imperil one's soul.

The Catholic church considers St. John Chrysostom one of its great ones, a saint. He has become known to religious history as the golden-mouthed orator. Fr. Edward Flannery, in his book *The Anguish of the Jews*, says that St. John Chrysostom, "even in an age in which rhetorical denunciation [of Jews] was often indulged with complete abandon" unhappily "dwarfed" everyone else's record. Here are words of the fourth-century orator as quoted by Fr. Flannery:

How can Christians dare "have the slightest converse" with Jews, "most miserable of all men" (Homily 4:1), men who are "...lustful, rapacious, greedy, perfidious bandits." Are they not "inveterate murderers, destroyers, men possessed by the devil" whom "debauchery and drunkenness have given them the manners of the pig and the lusty goat. They know only one thing, to satisfy their gullets, get drunk, to kill and maim one another..." (1:4). Indeed, "they have surpassed the ferocity of wild beasts, for they murder their offspring and immolate them to the devil" (1:6). "They are impure and impious..." (1:4).

The Synagogue? Not only is it a theater and a house of prostitution, but a cavern of brigands, a "repair of wild beasts" (6:5), a place of "shame and ridicule" (1:3), "the domicile of the devil (1:6), as is also the souls of the Jews" (1:4, 6). Indeed Jews worship the devil; their rites are "criminal and impure"; their religion is "a disease" (3:1). Their synagogue, again, is "an assembly of criminals ... den of thieves ... a cavern of devils, an abyss of perdition" (1:2, 6:6).

[2] Quoted by Franklin Littell in *The Crucifixion of the Jews* (New York, 1975), p. 105.

God hates the Jews and always hated the Jews (6:4, 1:7), and on Judgment Day He will say to Judaizers, "Depart from Me, for you have had intercourse with My murderers." It is the duty of Christians to hate the Jews: "He who can never love Christ enough will never have done fighting against those [Jews] who hate Him" (7:1). Flee, then, their assemblies, flee their houses, and far from venerating the synagogue because of the books it contains hold it in hatred and aversion for the same reason" (1:5). Chrysostom himself gives the example: "... I hate the synagogue precisely because it has the law and prophets ... " (6:6). "... I hate the Jews also because they outrage the law. ... "[3]

These virulent assaults are part of a pattern of Christian anti-Semitism begun centuries before Chrysostom lived and continuing up to this very minute. They are a part of Christian history. If we believe in a sense of the mystical body, of what Teilhard de Chardin has named the noosphere (that membrane of consciousness that covers the universe, and in which we all partake), of the Collective Unconscious of Carl Gustav Jung (which gives the lie to the notion that we are born with a *tabula rasa*, a mind clean as a slate, ready to receive all totally new impressions) — if we have some grasp of any or all of these, then we must at least vaguely comprehend the company some see us in as historical crimes against the Jews are considered.

Given this, all of the foregoing, how many sermons, homilies, lectures about the Holocaust can any of us remember having heard in church? It is over half a century since World War II began. There have been over twenty-five hundred sermon/homily opportunities for each of us to hear *something* about one of the most significant events in all of human history. I, personally, have not heard one. I have heard preachings on why it is a sin for men to wear Bermuda shorts, for example, or the Easter bunny, but nothing even remotely hinting at the Holocaust.

The subject of this essay is precisely that. It is the Holocaust, begun with a capital letter because it is of a specific event that we write, a unique, one-time, never before event that is ignored by many of us perhaps because it was so terrible and because it is so painful for us to face up to.

The number of Christians who have looked perseveringly at the subject is frighteningly small. They are there, and not to be

---

[3] *The Anguish of the Jews* (New York, 1965), p. 48.

ignored. Some of them will be quoted in these pages. Nevertheless the awareness of the relationship between Christianity and the Holocaust must be spread so that all Christians will know what many Jews already know about Christianity, that unless Christianity is revitalized, and soon, it too may have been among the victims at Auschwitz. It is certainly necessary to remember, as Franklin Littell has underlined in his book *The Crucifixion of the Jews*, that Jesus and Paul and Peter would have perished at Auschwitz.

One problem with this vast subject is where to begin; another related difficulty is how to proceed. Perhaps a chronological approach to this history of Christian antiSemitism is the logical starting point. We can proceed from then to now and end with hopeful and necessary projections/suggestions for the future.

Early Christian AntiSemitism

We begin with earliest times. There was, indeed, antiSemitism in pre-Christian days. Some have seen the Exodus from Egypt by Israel as the first pogrom. That took place some twelve hundred years before Jesus' birth. About three centuries later the dispersion of Jews began, and through both forced and voluntary exile from Palestine Jewish communities could be found, before Christ, in Babylonia, the Mediterranean countries, Armenia, Persia, and Great Britain, among many nations. Problems with Greeks, Egyptians, Romans, and others have been documented by historians. Some of the famous names of the ancient past have berated Jews, men like Seneca, Cicero, Democritus, Tiberius, Trajan, Caligula, Quintilian, Juvenal, Tacitus — a list much too long.

However, it is Christian antiSemitism that must be elaborated here, a distinctly unique kind of attack on Judaism because of what has come to be known as the supersessionist theory. Briefly, this ideology contains the proclamation that the writings found in Jewish Scriptures have been fulfilled in Christianity. The people of the Book have been told that henceforth their Book is obsolete. How may Christians today consider that many Jews find the term "Old Testament" insulting?

Here is Fr. Flannery again:

> The first Christian Church, full of zeal and fervor, was a Jewish church in leadership, membership, and worship; and it remained within the

precincts of the Synagogue. But as the universalist implications of the Gospel message (not yet fully written) made themselves felt, a series of developments gradually brought this arrangement to an end. In the tones of a prophet, Stephen charged the people and their leaders with infidelity to Moses as well as to the Messiah (Acts 7:2–7:53). By private revelation, Peter was instructed to accept the demi-proselyte, Cornelius, into the Church without committing him to the Law (Acts 10). The council of the apostles at Jerusalem decreed that gentile converts were not to be held to the legal observances (Gal. 2; Acts 15:11). Paul preached the inefficacy of the Law for both Jew and gentiles (Rom. 1:16, 2:10–11). Finally, at Antioch, Paul confronted Peter, insisting that while Jewish Christians might practice the Law, faith in Jesus Christ was necessary and sufficient for salvation (Gal. 2:11–21). This was the final disposition of the matter. Judaeo-Christianity, thus rejected, was destined to become a snare to Christian and Jew alike and a source of conflict for both Church and Synagogue.[4]

St. Paul, it seems, did not have a predominantly divisive outlook. While he noted that the law was by way of preparation, and it was ended in Christ, he did not feel that God had somehow rejected Judaism. Rather, in Romans 11:28–29, Paul indicated that ". . . as the chosen people, [Jews] are still loved by God, loved for the sake of their ancestors. God never takes back his gifts or revokes his choice." But Paul has been interpreted to have said some harsh things about Jews, such as in 1 Thessalonians 2:13–16, and it is this latter attitude that has prevailed. This may be extremely unfair to Paul, as Norman Beck indicates in his valuable volume *Mature Christianity*, but this is how Paul has been generally understood through the centuries.

Littell points out that theological antiSemitism began with the gentile converts of many tribes, with their natural resentment of the priority of Israel, their resistance to the authority of events in Jewish history, their pride in their own ethnic values, languages, cultures. Soon Jews came to be regarded as hypocrites, professing a false religion. Other Christian scriptures have been cited to indicate anti-Jewish bias, particularly John's Gospel, but such interpretation appears to be clearly incorrect. Nevertheless, the influence of such misinterpretation seems to have been great. (It is, incidentally, in John 4:22 that we read these words of Jesus, not located in Matthew, Mark, or Luke: ". . . salvation comes from the Jews.")

---

[4]*The Anguish of the Jews,* p. 26.

Christian-Jewish hostility grew, with some persecutions conducted by Jews against members of the newer religion. However, these were comparatively insignificant, mainly reactionary.

Church teachers kept up the assault now begun. Ignatius of Antioch, who died at the beginning of the second century, required that no Christians could keep the Jewish Sabbath, but must, of course, observe the newly appointed Lord's Day of Christianity. Ignatius also condescended to brand the prophets of Israel as Christians before their time and not truly of the Jewish religion. This "takeover" is part of the supersessionist approach to the older scriptures.

Nils Dahl has written that "the simplistic doctrine that Israel was rejected and the church chosen to be a new people of God is not really found within the New Testament, although it is adumbrated in some of the late writings."[5] Rosemary Ruether disagrees. She insists, in *Faith and Fratricide*, that the church won historical existence for itself by negating and claiming to supersede the historical existence of Israel. Only a new Christology, Ruether believes, offers a way out of anti-Judaism for Christians.

The answer is not a clear one; indeed the question may not be. Nevertheless, what has proven to be historically evident is exemplified by the title of Jules Isaac's very important volume, published in 1964, *The Teaching of Contempt: The Christian Roots of Anti-Semitism*. Isaac was a French Jew, a historian, who lost his wife, daughter, and other family members in the Holocaust. He spent the final twenty-three years of his life studying the answer to the question of specifically Christian guilt in the massacre of the six million Jewish victims of the Holocaust. He concluded that a true Christian cannot be at once precisely that and anti-Jewish. However, he also concluded that antiSemitism is profoundly rooted in Christianity. Isaac wrote that from the time of early conflict with Judaism, the Christian church propagated three treacherous lies, what he calls the "three main themes of the teaching of contempt." They are (1) in the year A.D. 70 the dispersion of the Jews took place as a punishment by God for their infidelity; (2) at the time of Christ, Judaism was in an unhealthy, degenerate state; (3) the Jewish people are guilty of having killed God. To see how this third teaching has persisted we need only to read Michael Dov Weissmandl's ac-

---

[5] In Michael B. McGarry, *Christology after Auschwitz* (New York, 1977), p. 7.

count of a conversation with a papal nuncio in 1944, at the height of the Holocaust persecutions, wherein the church official is reported to have said this: "There is no innocent blood of Jewish children in the world. All Jewish blood is guilty. You have to die. This is the punishment that has been awaiting you because of that sin [deicide]."[6]

St. Justin was probably the first to proclaim that because Jews killed Christ, they had been made to suffer. He said to a rabbi that the "tribulations were justly imposed upon you, for you have murdered the Just One." This bad theology and bad history have been promulgated ever since by people calling themselves Christians.

In the third century St. Cyprian proved equally as anti-Judaic. First he says that Jesus was put to death by the Jews and then insists that "now the peoplehood of the Jews has been cancelled," a statement that could be used to justify the intimidation and even slaughter of Jews for seventeen more centuries. Another third-century figure, also sainted, Hippolytus, said that all that the Jews had done had been pardonable, but now they would be left in despair "because they killed the Son of their Benefactor."

In the fourth century there appear the first of three Western anti-Jewish policies as defined by Raul Hilberg in his volume *The Destruction of the European Jews*, namely conversion. (He notes, by the way, that while pre-Christian Rome crushed the independent Jewish state of Judea, Rome had no anti-Jewish policy and in fact Jews who lived in Rome itself enjoyed equality under the law.) Hilberg says that at this point the state began to carry out the anti-Jewish designs of the church, and continued to do so for twelve centuries. (The other two policies of the West applied against Jewry are expulsion — which began as an alternative but developed into a goal of antiSemitic activity — and the final policy as starkly put: to kill the Jews.) In Hilberg's words: "To summarize: Since the fourth century after Christ, there have been three anti-Jewish policies: conversion, expulsion, annihilation. The second appeared as an alternative to the first, and the third emerged as an alternative to the second."[7]

[6]Quoted by Irving Greenberg in "Judaism and Christianity after the Holocaust," in *Journal of Ecumenical Studies* 12 (Fall 1975), p. 526.

[7]*The Destruction of the European Jews* (New York, 1973), p. 3.

This fourth century, which Fr. Flannery calls "critical" in Jewish-Christian history, is filled with abusive attacks by churchmen. This was the time when Christianity became the state religion and came to have heavy political clout.

Eusebius of Caesarea distinguished between Hebrews (seen as primitive Christians) and Jews (less enlightened). The patriarchs were considered to be in the former group in this "displacement," or supersessionist, view. Hilary of Poitiers saw Jewish history as proof that the Jews are perpetually perverse. St. Ephraim called the Synagogue a "harlot," while Cyril of Jerusalem and Epiphanius, each with the honored title of saint, also wrote pejoratively about Jews. Another saint, Gregory of Nyssa, called Jews "slayers of the Lord, murderers of the prophets, enemies of God, haters of God, adversaries of grace, enemies of their fathers' faith, advocates of the devil, brood of vipers, slanderers, scoffers, men of darkened minds, leaven of the Pharisees, congregation of demons, sinners, wicked men, stoners, and haters of goodness."[8] St. Jerome continues the attack, seeing Jews as "serpents," contending that their image is found in Judas and their psalms and prayers are "the braying of donkeys."

In this atmosphere of hatred lived and preached John Chrysostom, characterized by Flannery as a man "who, up to his time, stands without peer or parallel in the entire literature *Adversus Judaeos*." As Flannery concludes, "Christians as well as Jews can only deplore these sermons."[9] St. Augustine saw the Jews as existing to serve Christians.

Other significant anti-Jewish developments during this period included church councils that prohibited Christians from marrying Jews and barred Christians from celebrating the Passover with Jews. There were some measures promulgated to assist Jews to preserve certain rights but these were restrained in comparison with what was preached and practiced against Jews. In effect many were forced out of agriculture and industry and into small trades. None could participate in public functions, the military, or administrative positions. At this time, too, physical attacks against Jews increased, involving the citizenry in anti-Jewish activity consistent with the anti-Jewish invective of the church Fathers.

---

[8] Flannery, *The Anguish of the Jews*, p. 47.
[9] Ibid., p. 49.

The Middle Ages

Later came forced baptisms of Jews (though opposed by Pope St. Gregory and official church policy) and Judaism was increasingly seen by many as a corrupt religion. In seventh-century Spain children of Jews were baptized and taken from their parents for a Christian education. Expulsion of Jews became more common, and we are reminded of Hilberg's second policy of antiSemitism effected by Western civilization. Forced conversions, particularly in nations like France, became the rule. In the eighth and ninth centuries, under Pepin and Charlemagne, conditions improved for Jews and were particularly advanced under Charlemagne's son Louis the Pious.

This respite, however, did not last. The archbishop of Lyons, St. Abrogard, wrote a pair of treatises, the titles of which only partially indicate their virulence: *On the Insolence of Jews* and *On Jewish Superstitions*. By the tenth century, Jewish property began to be expropriated. Furthermore, a custom grew up where on Good Fridays, in retribution for the crucifixion, a local Jew received a symbolic blow on his face from a church official. Thus continued and passed on was the convenience of blaming others for the death of Jesus who, according to church teachings, died because all, *including Christians*, were sinners and thus all had responsibility in Jesus' death.

The end of the eleventh century, 1096 precisely, is a major catastrophic time in Jewish history. This was the year of the infamous First Crusade. Let us look at the Crusade from a Jewish point of view:

> The Crusades and their attendant degradation were firmly imprinted on the historic consciousness of the Jews. This period became singled out in the popular mind as the start of and explanation for the misfortunes of the Jews, although in fact the excesses were only symptomatic of a process which had already been set in motion earlier. The Crusades marked in various ways a turning point in the history of the Western world, and this was reflected also in Jewish history. Indeed, it is from this point only that the history of the Jews in the Rhineland and Central Europe may be said to acquire continuity; whereas before the general picture has had to be constructed from scattered fragments and documents, henceforth the record is more or less sustained and complete. As in the case to some extent with general historiography, it is only

at this period, with the remarkably graphic and moving records of the Rhineland massacres in 1096, that consistent Jewish historiography, or at least chronography, begins to be preserved, even though there are fragmentary records written earlier. The history that now unfolded was predominantly a tragic one. Whereas in European Jewish history before this date episodes of violence and persecution are occasionally known, there now began a period of intermittently recurring massacre and persecution which colored European Jewish experience for centuries to come. The heightened religiosity of the age resulted in the sharpening of the system of anti-Jewish discrimination and of Jewish humiliation, culminating in the legislation of the Fourth Lateran Council of 1215. The chronicles of Solomon b. Samson, Eliezer b. Nathan of Mainz, Ephraim b. Jacob of Bonn, Eleazar b. Judah of Worms, and many others whose names are not known, described the events of the Crusades, the scenes of the massacres, and the martyrs. They are also to be regarded as basic sources from which statistical accounts of the Crusades must start. Through capturing these events they magnified their significance, but thereby furnished an ideal of conduct which was constantly recalled to mind whenever severe persecutions befell the Jews.[10]

Note the clearly different emphasis of the article on the Crusades in the *Catholic Encyclopedia* from this, its concluding paragraph:

The Crusades represented an effort of the greatest magnitude. Christians in the Middle Ages consented to enormous sacrifices for what they regarded as a sacred obligation: the defense of their brethren in danger and the liberation of the Holy Land hallowed by the footsteps of Christ. The Crusades were not an act of intolerance: they aimed neither at the forced conversion of non-Christian nor at the massacre of "infidels." These expeditions had, indeed, military, financial, and economical aspects, but above all else they can be characterized as a penitential act and voluntary effort in the service of God. The notion of bearing arms in God's service, though it may seem paradoxical, was perfectly attuned to the mentality of the Middle Ages and, in the last analysis, assured the success of the Crusades. The concept of devoting considerable effort to a task in the service of God guarantees lasting favor to the Crusade idea as applied in our day to the works of peace.

The thirteenth-century Doctor of the Church, St. Thomas Aquinas, wrote this: "It would be licit, according to custom, to hold Jews,

---

[10]*Encyclopedia Judaica.*

because of their crime, in perpetual servitude, and therefore the princes may regard the possessions of Jews as belonging to their state; however they may use them with moderation and not deprive Jews of things necessary to life."[11] Later, this became law. As one jurist wrote, "The Jew cannot have anything of his own. Whatever he acquires he acquires not for himself but for the king."[12] By the end of the thirteenth century Jews were forced out of France, England, and most of Germany.

The next dismal chapter is one of the most unbelievable of all. It is the period that brought on the accusation of what is called "ritual murder." The charge seems to have been first seriously aimed at Jews in the twelfth century. Ritual murder, initially, was said to be the sacrifice by Jews of a Christian victim, usually a child, during the Christian Holy Week, for religious purposes. But this was too restrictive. Soon, any murder of a Christian that was determined to be for some supernatural end was considered in this category. The first charge occurred in England but it spread to several European nations. Many Jews were massacred in retaliation. Some of the Christian "victims" became, without foundation, popularly venerated by other Christians. The finding of a dead Christian child, regardless of circumstances, might be enough to raise the collective Christian voice of a community against Jews. Actually, such accusations against Jews were absurd, given Jewish doctrine and practice, which included an abomination of bloodletting, and at least four popes insisted on the innocence of Jews of these practices. Who could believe it? A Catholic priest and historian, Fr. Vacandard, has established that not a single case of ritual murder has ever been historically proven.[13] But the denunciations, incredible as they were, continued.

Pope Innocent III's Fourth Lateran Council decreed that Jews (and Saracens) had to wear distinctive clothing, a full seven and a half centuries before the Nazis required the yellow star as Jewish garb. The Talmud was burned by Christians, people were threatened with excommunication for consulting Jewish physicians, and perhaps a hundred thousand Jews were killed in Germany and Austria in 1298 because of the unfounded charge that a Jew had desecrated a communion host. Tales of smaller scale massacres

---

[11]Flannery, *The Anguish of the Jews*, p. 95.
[12]Ibid.
[13]Ibid., p. 100.

abound, and many Jews, faced with forced baptism, chose suicide rather than betray their faith. In the fifteenth century, another saint, the Franciscan John Capistrano, *earned* his title "scourge of the Jews" and he became one of the Inquisitors of the Jews. The Inquisition, of course, has been seen, finally, as one of the most tragic periods in Christianity's history.

In about the middle of the twelfth century, Christians came to believe increasingly in the efficacy of force to gain ecclesiastical unity. It reached such a point that in several regions, the death penalty was decreed for heresy. Because he feared the charge of heresy would be abused for political motives, Pope Gregory IX, in 1231, required that only the church could try heretics, and he then instituted the papal Inquisition. The officials had great power, not the least of which was the naming of deputies who shared in that power. Since political rulers could themselves be denounced, the Inquisition was widely supported by the civil authorities. Death penalties, sometimes preceded by extreme tortures, were administered against victims. Jews who had been forced to be baptized but remained loyal to Judaism were persecuted, particularly in Spain, through the Inquisition. In Spain the oppression was especially widespread and caused much anguish even to Jews who had not converted and were technically outside of the Inquisition's domain.

From Luther to de Gobineau

The Reformation period followed — with little improvement, at least in attitude by Christians toward the Jews.

In the sixteenth century, Pope Paul IV acted in such a way that Flannery judged that "there are few popes who compare with him for severity toward Jews."[14] In 1700 Johann Eisenmenger published *Entdectes Judentum* (Judaism Unmasked), which has been an inspired encyclopedia of antiSemitism since its appearance.

For various reasons Jews moved into ghettos and were separated from the rest of the citizens. In some areas this actually led to their protection and helped their survival, although this was not the intent of those who decreed and enforced the ghettoizations. But as time passed, many ghettos began to pass also, and as the nineteenth century opened, emancipation of Jews became

---

[14]Flannery, *The Anguish of the Jews*, p. 154.

a gradual reality. The reasons are complex and irrelevant for our purposes. Some were of an internal, Jewish nature, while others had a broader basis. The French and American revolutions are important here. But antiSemitism was not absent. German thinkers like Friedrich Schleiermacher, Johann Fichte, and Johann Wolfgang von Goethe were vocal about their negative attitudes toward Jews, and the influential Karl Marx, himself born a Jew but baptized as a child, wrote this:

> What is the object of the Jew's worship in this world? Usury. What is his worldly God? Money. Very well then; emancipation from usury and money, that is, from practical, real Judaism, would constitute the emancipation of our time. . . . The emancipation of society from Jewry.[15]

Nevertheless the cause of political emancipation of Jews was advanced in the world. But, as Flannery indicates, while this was an important improvement in the situation of Jews, the blessing was not unaccompanied by certain reversals. "Instead of disappearing, antiSemitism merely changed its guise. An old form was on the wane, another in the making. The theological bias was fainter but the national, economic, and ethnic resentments were stronger. Less noted as a 'deicide people,' Jews became abhorred as supposedly unassimilable economic parasites. Clearly, their emancipation had a proviso attached: that they dissolve in the gentile melting pot."[16]

Of course the chronology suggested here is too neat to be entirely accurate. Non-theological antiSemitism may be said to have begun as early as two centuries previously, in the seventeenth. Names like Baruch Spinoza, himself a Jew, Voltaire, Diderot, Hegel, Proudhon, and many others must be listed. One of the most infamous of all, Arthur de Gobineau, in his *Essay on the Inequality of Human Races*, advocated Aryan supremacy and Semitic inferiority. Jews, in de Gobineau's view, were especially inferior to German Aryans. His essay was published in 1884. In just half a century, Hitler would try to purge the world of these inferior beings and de Gobineau's "scientific" findings were among the foundation points of the Führer's policy. Nor was de Gobineau alone in his teachings, nor Germany alone infected by such thought. In France the infa-

---

[15] Flannery, *The Anguish of the Jews*, p. 67.
[16] Ibid., p. 173.

mous Dreyfus affair of 1894, in which a Jewish officer was framed as a German spy, brought antiSemitism into the open again. Although the perpetrators of the crime were exposed (one who forged documents implicating Dreyfus committed suicide), and although Dreyfus was ultimately and absolutely cleared (not without extreme difficulties), latent antiSemitism became open. Catholics in France, as symbolized by the Catholic press of that nation, disgraced themselves by their show of anti-Jewish feelings catalyzed by the Dreyfus case.

The Twentieth Century

The time was opportune then, for the publication in 1905 of a book called *The Protocols of the Learned Elders of Zion*. This volume is purported to be a series of two dozen lectures by influential Jews on how to subjugate the world to Jewish control — the international Jewish conspiracy hoax, if you will. *The Protocols* was proven to be a forgery, but became very influential. It was promoted as true by Henry Ford and has even been cited recently by certain Arab diplomats in the United Nations as evidence of a Jewish plot to take over the world. The exposure of the fraud came in 1921, but to this hour *The Protocols* remains fodder for certain antiSemites who refuse to recognize the truth on this matter.

World War I proved tragic for Jews. While they fought in the armies of their respective nations, they were not trusted, and, predictably, when the war ended, they were branded as unwilling participants, particularly (and unjustly) in Germany. Polish armies probably murdered some thirty thousand Jews (President Woodrow Wilson interceded to help stop the slaughter), two hundred thousand Rumanian Jews lost their citizenship, and in Hungary, Austria, and Turkey Jews were separated from other citizens.

How were they to react, then, when Hitler's onslaught began? To whom could they turn for assistance, for compassion? They were left almost entirely isolated and helpless. As Raul Hilberg has shrewdly indicated about this period, Hitler did not have to originate any propaganda or invent any laws. He did not have to create a machine. All he had to do was rise to personal power. The stage was, indeed, set for him. All it needed was a star performer. German Cardinal Michael von Faulhaber, in a 1933 sermon, that gave inaccurate theological support to so much of the prejudice against Jews said:

> After the death of Christ Israel was dismissed from the service of Revelation. She did not know the time of her visitation. She had repudiated and rejected the Lord's Anointed, had driven him to the Cross. . . . The Daughters of Zion received the bill of divorce and from that time forth Assuerus wanders, forever restless, over the face of the earth.[17]

Actually, however, it appears that as we approach the period of the Holocaust religious antiSemitism was less destructive than the racial kind. We in no way mean to mitigate our denunciation of any form of such hatred, but it is interesting to note the major line of discussion in a book by the Jewish scholar Uriel Tal, *Christians and Jews in Germany: Religion, Politics, and Ideology in the Second Reich, 1870–1914*. Here, basically, although caricatured, are Professor Tal's conclusions: Tension arose from the unwillingness of Germans to allow Jews to be integrated into the state while Jews attempted, at the same time, to retain a certain separateness. From a theological viewpoint, Judaism was seen as an anachronism, replaced by the New Dispensation. Liberal Jews felt that liberal Protestants really accepted Judaism's basic opposition to Christianity and reduced religion to ethics, reduced theological mysteries to anthropology, therefore denying the dogma of the church. As Tal wrote, it is clear that it was the non-Christian and anti-Christian character of racial-political anti-Judaism that proved to be the greatest obstacle to its development. After World War I, however, the non-Christian anti-Christian character of antiSemitism grew stronger, and this removed a main obstacle to the spread of *racial* antiSemitism.

Tal continues by saying that Christian antiSemitism was not as virulent as its racial counterpart. It permitted Jews to exist (though not flourish) as the living witness to the truth of Christianity. The Jew has to remain in order to act out the role of villain in the drama of salvation, and the Jew could, after all, be converted, baptized. But according to racial antiSemitism, nothing could penetrate the tainted Jewish seed. The Jew must be destroyed. Racial anti-Semitism put its faith in the efficacy of blood. It is important to Tal's thesis to note that, while racial antiSemitism was a worse brand, the history of Christianity provided the rationale for vio-

---

[17]McGarry, *Christology after Auschwitz*, p. 4.

lence against Jews. We are ready, now, to consider the third of the Western policies against the Jews, according to Hilberg. Kill them.

Jews have asked, and continue to ask: Where was God at Auschwitz? Why aren't more Christians asking that question, too? Jewish survivor Elie Wiesel told me in a television interview that he believes that "the sincere Christian knows that what died in Auschwitz was not the Jewish people but Christianity." Wiesel went on to say that Pope John XXIII, whom Wiesel knew, saw this and therefore called the Second Vatican Council into existence — perhaps Wiesel would say in an attempt at a resurrection.

In viewing what theologian Robert E. Willis called "the indisputable success of the Nazi program" Arthur Hertzberg has asked, ". . . is it conceivable that the enormous power of this hatred was bred in a few short decades?"[18] The answer is obvious. We, as inheritors of the traditions of the members of the Mystical Body, as participants in the noosphere, as constituents of the Collective Unconscious, must recognize this.

Perhaps, for a period at least, we need to modify a traditional question as we try to gain perspective on history, on events. Many of us have been taught to judge relevance by asking: What is this in the light of eternity? For a time, let us put it this way: What is this in the light of the flames of Auschwitz, when humanity ratified Hell?

---

[18]Robert E. Willis, "Christian Theology after Auschwitz," *Journal of Ecumenical Studies* 12 (Fall 1975), p. 495.

Chapter 2

The Nazi Atrocities

Jewish theologian Irving Greenberg regards the Holocaust as an unprecedented challenge to both Judaism and Christianity. It radically contradicts, he believes, the central affirmation of both faiths. In the light of the great cruelties of World War II, and particularly of the attempted annihilation of a people, how can we say that we are made in God's image? How can we believe that human life is infinitely precious? "Both religions have always sought to isolate their central events — Exodus and Easter — from further revelations or from the challenge of the demonic counter-experience of evil in history. By and large, both religions have continued since 1945 as if nothing had happened to change their central understanding. It is increasingly obvious that this is impossible, that the Holocaust cannot be ignored."[1]

We have mentioned that the Nazi attitude was a giant step of logical progression based on a long and sorrowful history of political, religious, and racial antiSemitism. But even the Nazi tactics were not very original. Nazis demanded the protection of Aryan blood from defilement by Jewish blood. But the Synod of Elvira, in the year 306, prohibited intermarriage and sexual intercourse between Christians and Jews. In 535 the Synod of Clermont decreed that Jews could not hold public office. In 538 Jews were forbidden to show themselves in the streets during Passion Week.

---

[1]In Eva Fleischner, ed., *Auschwitz: Beginning of a New Era?* (New York, 1977), p. 8.

The list is long, the list is embarrassing: Jews were not permitted to take Christians to court or be witnesses against Christians in a trial (1179); Jewish clothes had to be marked with a badge (1215); there was compulsory ghettoization of Jews (1267); Christians could not engage in real estate transactions with Jews (1279); Jews were not allowed to earn academic degrees (1434). This is only a partial roster of policies that have their parallels in Nazi practices.

There were, as we know, theoretical bases used to rationalize what was to be done. There was *Rassenkunde*, racial science, based primarily on the work of Arthur de Gobineau (d. 1882) who insisted that the racial question overshadows all other problems of history, that it holds the key to them all, and that the inequality of the races explains the whole course of a people's destiny. Johann Fichte (d. 1814) has been called the father of both German nationalism and modern German antiSemitism. German composer Richard Wagner (d. 1883) held racist concepts influenced by de Gobineau (who was French) and Houston Steward Chamberlain (who was English). Wagner was pleased to learn from the former that the Germans were probably the best of all the Aryans, and from the latter that Jewish influence could best be combated through Teutonic cultural development. Chamberlain also argued that the Germans had the inalienable right to be masters of the world. Wagner was a strong, unrelenting Jewhater best characterized, perhaps, by this statement: "The Jew is the plastic demon of the decline of mankind." There was also the influence of social Darwinism on Nazi theory, and of Goethe's Faust, with his overreaching will, as Nora Levin has indicated.[2]

In 1925–27, when the German Republic was relatively stable, rioting against Jews grew, as did the desecration of Jewish cemeteries. Legislation against Jews was constantly introduced in the national and local legislatures. During this period over seven hundred racist, anti-Jewish newspapers were published throughout the country. Even in children's books passages like this could be read: "Without solution of the Jewish question / No salvation of mankind."

---

[2]*The Holocaust* (New York, 1973), pp. 7–8.

The Rise of Adolf Hitler

The portrait of the Jew that emerged from all of this was clearly contradictory. On one side the Jew was presented as subhuman, as contemptible, as a mere pestilence to be eradicated. However, the second view, of the Jew as "the mythic omnipotent superadversary" was also promulgated. It seemed to be an either/or situation, but it was not. In either instance, facing the Jew as disease or the Jew as superenemy, something needed to be done. Someone was needed who would lead the fight against the Jew. Onto the scene came a redeemer. After a humiliating loss in the First World War (blamed on Jews by some) and an even more humiliating peace treaty, the person who could convince a significant number of Germans that he would unite Germany, return to it a rightful prestige, and at the same time rid it of the cause of its troubles — the Jews — would be regarded as a savior. Onto the scene came Adolf Hitler. Here was the magnetic personality who could convince people that "by defending myself against the Jew, I am fighting for the work of the Lord." Here was the man of whom a German Christian, a Dr. Engelke, had said, "God has manifested himself not in Jesus Christ but in Adolf Hitler." Hanns Kerrl, Minister for Church Affairs, stated in 1937: "A new authority has risen as to what Christ and Christianity really are — Adolf Hitler." Kerrl even went beyond this. "As Christ in his twelve disciples raised a stock fortified unto martyrdom, so in Germany today we are witnessing the same thing. . . . Adolf Hitler is the true Holy Ghost!"[3]

Hitler was born in 1889 in Austria. He proved a poor student and his academic failures irritated him for many succeeding years. He enjoyed reading the Nordic tales of gods and heroes and particularly was addicted to the writings of Karl May, an ex-convict author who had never been to the U.S. Wild West but who wrote action tales set in that region. These works featured a hero called Old Shatterhand, an American who thrived on killing Indians who, he considered, were members of an inferior race. Hitler was to model himself after Old Shatterhand. It is known that Hitler continued to read May's literature (which was aimed at a juvenile audience) while conducting the war against Russia, and he sometimes referred to the Soviets as "Redskins." The future Führer fought in

[3]Peter Viereck, *Metapolitics* (New York, 1961), p. 289.

World War I, was seriously wounded and received several decorations. In 1919, when the German Worker's Party was founded,
he became its fifty-fifth member. Before long he was appointed
its head of propaganda and publicity. And he showed himself
to be an especially effective speaker. Early in 1921 the first great
Nazi mass meeting was held in Munich, and Hitler was made first
chairman of the National Socialist German Workers' Party (NS-
DAP). Some three months later, on November 4, 1921, a private
army, the SA (storm troopers) was instituted. Descriptively identified as the Brownshirts, these guards at Nazi meetings were later
used to battle Communists and others in the streets. By 1932 there
were four hundred thousand men in the SA.

In late 1923 Hitler made a move to seize power in Bavaria with
the so-called Beer Hall *Putsch* in Munich. This attempted coup
failed, and Hitler was arrested, tried, and convicted. During the
trial, the defendant made a deep impression on certain Germans
before he was sentenced to five years in prison (of which he served
eight and a half months). It was while imprisoned that be began
dictating his book, *Mein Kampf* (My Fight), to friends. Millions of
copies were sold throughout the world and Hitler became rich on
the royalties.

Here, for our purposes, are some brief selections from *Mein
Kampf* (New York, 1971): The Jews' "whole existence is an em-
bodied protest against the aesthetics of the Lord's image" (p. 178).
"Was there any form of filth or profligacy, particularly in cultural
life, without at least one Jew involved in it?" (p. 57). "The fore-
most connoisseurs of this truth regarding the possibilities in the use
of falsehood and slander have always been the Jews; for after all,
their whole existence is based on one single great lie, to wit, that
they are a religious community while actually they are a race —
and what a race!" (p. 232). "Existence impels the Jew to lie, and to
lie perpetually, just as it compels the inhabitants of the northern
countries to wear warm clothing" (p. 305). "The Jew has always
been a people with definite racial characteristics and never a religion; only in order to get ahead he early sought for a means which
could distract unpleasant attention from his person" (p. 306).

Hitler cites the fraudulent *Protocols of the Learned Elders of Zion*
to support his case, he rants against pacifism as "Jewish nonsense,"
he insists that no Jew could be a German and Jews are inferior beings. His attack became so broad that Hitler confidently wrote:

"And so the Jew today is the great agitator for the complete destruction of Germany. Wherever in the world we read of attacks
against Germany, Jews are their fabricators, just as in peacetime
and during War the press of the Jewish stock exchange and Marx-
ists systematically stirred up hatred against Germany until state
after state abandoned neutrality and, renouncing the true inter-
ests of the peoples, entered the service of the World War coalition"
against Germany (p. 623).

Hitler left prison in December 1924. In elections less than three
months later, a reconstituted NSDAP gained fewer than a quarter
of a million votes out of twenty-seven million cast. A month later
Field Marshall Paul von Hindenburg became the second President
of the Weimar Republic. The next year, a Party day was held in
Nuremberg at which 30,000 Brownshirts marched. In 1928, in
Reichstag elections, Nazis, as the NSDAP was called, gained only
2.5 percent of the vote. In early 1929, Heinrich Himmler became
head of Hitler's blackshirted personal guard — the SS, or elite
guard. In August of the same year, Party day attracted 150,000
participants. The next year, in Reichstag elections, the Nazi share
of votes rose to 18 percent; SS and SA activities grew more bold.

In presidential elections in 1932, Hitler received 13.7 million
votes. Hindenburg was reelected president of the Republic, and
on January 30th of the next year Hitler was appointed chancellor of
the Republic. Soon he gained emergency powers by presidential
decree, and in new elections Nazis claimed 288 seats out of 647.
Himmler and Joseph Goebbels grew in power as did Rudolf Hess.
On April 26 (1933) the Gestapo force was formed. In November
of that year the Nazi party received 93 percent of the vote cast in
the Reichstag election. In August 1934, President von Hindenburg
died. Hitler declared himself the Führer of Germany, a move ratified by a vote of approval of nearly 90 percent of those casting
ballots less than three weeks afterwards.

A year later, official steps were taken to disenfranchise Jews in
what have become known as the Nuremberg Laws on Citizenship
and Race. Louis L. Snyder describes these laws:

> The Nuremberg Laws were designed by Hitler to define the status of
> Jews in Germany and to restrict them in political and social life. In
> his drive for political power Hitler promoted a bitter antiSemitic cam-
> paign and stirred up extreme hatred against the Jews. After becoming

Chancellor, he encouraged his followers to assault and beat Jews, to humiliate them by forcing them to clean the streets, to picket or close Jewish businesses, and to denounce Jews in the professions as rogues, profiteers, and traitors. When accounts of Nazi atrocities were published abroad, a boycott of German goods was urged in retaliation. The result was disastrous for German Jews. Jewish businesses were boycotted, Jewish physicians excluded from hospitals, Jewish judges dismissed, and Jewish students thrown out of the universities. Jews were increasingly barred from all German life. "The Jew can speak only Jewish. When he writes in German, he lies." From September to November 1935 Hitler took steps to define the legal status of Jews in Germany. The Nuremberg Laws withdrew German citizenship from persons of "non-German blood."[4]

Hitler Unopposed

German audacity continued to increase. So did that of Italy, and during 1936 the two nations grew together on an official level. In 1937 Pope Pius XI was concerned enough to issue an encyclical letter, "With Deep Anxiety," which protested German violations of natural law and justice. This letter was not a strong statement on behalf of Jews, and historians have lamented this. What is little known, however, is that another statement had been planned, *and in fact was written* for Pius XI, which could have changed the history of World War II.

The *National Catholic Reporter*, first broke the tragic story about an unpublished papal encyclical letter on antiSemitism, a letter which, had it been circulated, might have had an immense effect on the prosecution and persecutions of World War II. Pope Pius XI commissioned a U.S. Jesuit priest, John LaFarge, to write an encyclical for the Pope, attacking racism and antiSemitism. The request was made in June 1938, a full fifteen months before the outbreak of the Second World War. Through a series of apparently Machiavellian machinations, the message never got into print. After examining the evidence, an editorial writer for the *National Catholic Reporter* indicated that, "Considering all this, we must conclude that the publication of the encyclical draft at the time it was written may have saved hundreds of thousands, perhaps millions, of lives."

---

[4]*Encyclopedia of the Third Reich* (New York, 1976), p. 252.

I wish I could say the story is incredible. But I have read church history and it is all *too* believable. Fr. LaFarge wrote *Humani Generis Unitas* (The Unity of the Human Race) as requested, but apparently his Jesuit superior general, a Polish count, Fr. Wlodimir Ledochowski, withheld the completed manuscript from the Pope for what *NCR* concluded were "political reasons." Pius XI's death the following February doomed the declaration on antiSemitism to limbo. (Cardinal Jean Tisserant, a close associate of the pope, claimed that Pius XI was poisoned by a physician, Dr. Francesco Petacci, whose daughter Clara was Mussolini's mistress. The pope died on the eve of a scheduled speech to Italian bishops which was to have been an attack on Fascism.) When his successor, Pope Pius XII, published his first encyclical — using the title of LaFarge's work — the sections on racism and antiSemitism were not included. Here is Jim Castelli's account in the *NCR*:

> The anti-Semitism section entitled "The Jews and Anti-Semitism (Religious Separation)" directly follows the racism section. It begins by saying, "It becomes clear that the struggle for racial purity ends by being uniquely the struggle against Jews."

The encyclical draft said contemporary antiSemitism has historical roots:

> Save for the systematic cruelty, this struggle, in true motives and methods, is no different from persecutions everywhere carried out against the Jews from antiquity. These persecutions have been censured by the Holy See on more than one occasion, but especially when they have worn the mantle of Christianity.

The following paragraphs described the "actual persecution of the Jews":

> As a result of such a persecution, millions of persons are deprived of the most elementary rights and privileges of citizens in the very land of their birth. Denied legal protection against violence and robbery, exposed to every form of insult and public degradation, innocent people are treated as criminals though they have circumspectly obeyed the law of their native land.
>   Even those who in time of war fought bravely for their country are treated as traitors, and the children of those who laid down their

lives in their country's behalf are branded as outlaws by the very fact of their parentage. The values of patriotism, so loudly invoked for the benefit of one class of citizens, are ridiculed when invoked for others who come under the racial ban.

In the case of the Jews, this flagrant denial of human rights sends many thousands of helpless persons out over the face of the earth without any resources. . . .

Another Catholic lay publication, the magazine *Commonweal*, editorialized about the scandal:

. . . there is no evading the past; it is true that many Christians were all-too-ready to co-operate in the persecution of the Jews, and it is this fact, even more than the silence of Pius XII, that stains the collective conscience of Christians. History is dealing harshly with Pius XII on this issue and rightly so, but on this side of the Atlantic as well as the other he was not alone in keeping silence.[5]

Too many people remained silent, perhaps did not want to get involved. The charge weighs heavily against first German and later many other intellectuals. Nora Levin has written of "the general world indifference that prevailed through the agony of Europe's Jews."[6] We know that there was no significant protest; a German battlecry became famous: "Hep! Hep! Hep! Death and Destruction to all the Jews." Few reacted negatively to the slogan "The Jews are our misfortune." There was little outcry when the Nazi's chanted, "Germany wake up, Judah drop dead." There is no record of a serious protest to the vicious words found in the SA *Sturmlied:* "and when Jewish blood spurts from the knife, things will go twice as well." On at least five occasions, Hitler said these words: "Today I will once more be a prophet. If the international Jewish financiers inside and outside Europe should again succeed in plunging the nations into a world war, the result will be . . . the annihilation of the Jewish race throughout Europe."

Levin has indicated an atmosphere of non-involvement in German politics in the second quarter of this century. "As democracy had been held in contempt as a decadent, Western notion, the

---

[5]Cf. *Harry James Cargas in Conversation with Elie Wiesel* (New York, 1976), pp. 40–42.

[6]*The Holocaust*, p. 143.

Germans of the Weimar period developed no taste for citizen participation in political life and consequently, gained no experience. Politics generally was dismissed as hypocritical and compromising and few men wanted to be sullied by it. Decisions were left to authorities while the people of the nation looked on passively."[7]

Lest there be an erroneous impression given, however, we must not overlook the active role that German scholarship had in supporting Hitler. Many believe that protest, particularly by religious and intellectual groups, could have shaken Hitler's determination about Jews. There is evidence of this from the reaction to Hitler's euthanasia program, which in two years killed some fifty thousand sick persons, people who were judged insane, infirm, or in some other way unproductive citizens. Some religious figures spoke out and wrote against the measures. As Levin has indicated, and others concur: "Church protests continued and popular opposition mounted until Hitler had to discontinue the program."[8] Such a reaction was not in evidence, however, over the increasingly harsh treatment of German Jews. And so World War II began with people concerned about territory, about honor, about self-purification. Historian Lucy S. Dawidowicz put another construction on the events and illustratively titled her book *The War Against the Jews 1933–1945.*

Death Camps

What were Jews subject to before the Nazis and others implemented a plan of "Final Solution"? One statistic may give an idea. From 1932 to 1934 Jews in Germany had a suicide rate 50 percent higher than that of non-Jews. Concentration camps appeared in 1933; by the end of that year there were fifty. Harassment and beatings of Jews continued and grew in frequency and ferocity, culminating in *Crystal Night*, a brief period of organized terror (November 9–10, 1938) in which the destruction of 76 synagogues, 171 Jewish homes, and 815 Jewish shops was reported by Reinhard Heydrich to Goering. Another 191 synagogues had been set on fire and 36 Jews were murdered. This organized, concerted effort also resulted in the arrest and incarceration of 20,000 Jews. On the day following, 680 Jews committed suicide.

---

[7] *The Holocaust*, pp. 22–23.
[8] Ibid., p. 304.

Jewish children were tormented by other students as well as by teachers and school administrators. Boycotts of Jewish businesses were effected. Jews had to be identified as Jews on their passports. Expropriation of property and imprisonment — including the separation of families — became highly common.

All of this led to the death camps, the camps that after the war so many people claimed not to know about. We may ask again as we consider what went on there: Who designed them? Who built them? Who operated them? Who tortured and murdered in them? Many who did these things called themselves Christians. What implication does this have for those of us who now call ourselves Christians?

What exactly went on in the death camps? Here is how Adolf Eichmann, the master killer from the "master race," describes an event in his career. He tells of seeing his first Jewish execution at Minsk:

> I was sent by my immediate superior, General Muller. . . . He liked to send me around on his behalf. I was in effect a traveling salesman for the Gestapo, just as I once had been a traveling salesman for an oil company in Austria.
>
> Muller had heard that Jews were being shot near Minsk and wanted a report. . . . They had already started, so I could see only the finish. Although I was wearing a leather coat which reached almost to my ankles, it was very cold. I watched the last group of Jews undress, down to their shirts. They walked the last 100 or 200 yards — they were not driven — then they jumped into the pit. It was impressive to see them all jumping into the pit without offering any resistance whatsoever. Then the men of the squad banged away into the pit with their rifles and machine pistols.
>
> Why did that scene linger so long in my memory? Perhaps because I had children myself. And there were children in that pit. I saw a woman hold a child of a year or two into the air, pleading. At that moment all I wanted to say was, "Don't shoot, hand over the child." Then the child was hit. I was so close that later I found bits of brains splattered on my long leather coat. My driver helped me remove them. Then we returned to Berlin.[9]

Here is the testimony of a Polish guard at Auschwitz, given at the Nuremberg trial:

---

[9]Levin, *The Holocaust*, pp. 291–292.

WITNESS: . . . women carrying children were [always] sent with them to the crematorium. [Children were of no labor value so they were killed. The mothers were sent along, too, because separation might lead to panic, hysteria — which might slow up the destruction process, and this could not be afforded. It was simpler to condemn the mothers too and keep things quiet and smooth.] The children were then torn from their parents outside the crematorium and sent to the gas chambers separately. [At that point, crowding more people into the gas chambers became the most urgent consideration. Separating meant that more children could be packed in separately, or they could be thrown in over the heads of adults once the chamber was packed.] When the extermination of the Jews in the gas chambers was at its height, orders were issued that children were to be thrown straight into the crematorium furnaces, or into pits near the crematorium, without being gassed first.

SMIRNOV (Russian prosecutor): How am I to understand this? Did they throw them into the fire alive, or did they kill them first?

WITNESS: They threw them in alive. Their screams could be heard at the camp. It is difficult to say how many children were destroyed in this way.

SMIRNOV: Why did they do this?

WITNESS: It's very difficult to say. We don't know whether they wanted to economize on gas, or if it was because there was not enough room in the gas chambers.[10]

Rudolf Hoess, the commander at Auschwitz, who confessed that "I personally arranged the gassing of two million persons between June–July 1941 and the end of 1943," recalled this in his memoirs: "I remember, too, a woman who tried to throw her children out of the gas chamber, just as the door was closing. Weeping, she called out: 'At least let my precious children live.' There were many such scenes which affected all who witnessed them."[11]

   One account, as one author describes it, "froze the Nuremberg Court with pity and horror."

On 5 October 1942, when I visited the building office, . . . my foreman Hubert Moennikes . . . told me that in the vicinity of the site, Jews from Dubno had been shot in three large pits, each about 30 meters long and

----

   [10]Quoted by Irving Greenberg in "Judaism and Christianity after the Holocaust," *Journal of Ecumenical Studies* 12 (Fall 1975), p. 524.
   [11]*Commandant at Auschwitz* (New York, 1961), pp. 140–141.

3 meters deep. About 1,500 persons had been killed daily. All of the 5,000 Jews who had still been living in Dubno before the pogrom were to be liquidated. As the shootings had taken place in his presence he was still much upset.

Thereupon I drove to the site, accompanied by Moennikes and saw near it great mounds of earth, about 30 meters long and 2 meters high. Several trucks stood in front of the mounds. Armed Ukrainian militia drove the people off the trucks under the supervision of an S.S. man. The militia men acted as guards on the trucks and drove them to and from the pit. All these people had the regulation yellow patches on the front and back of their clothes, and thus could be recognized as Jews.

Moennikes and I went directly to the pits. Nobody bothered us. Now I heard rifle shots in quick succession, from behind one of the earth mounds. The people who had got off the trucks — men, women and children of all ages — had to undress upon the order of an S.S. man who carried a riding or dog whip. They had to put down their clothes in fixed places, sorted according to shoes, top clothing, and underclothing. I saw a heap of shoes of about 800 to 1,000 pairs, great piles of under-linen and clothing. Without screaming or weeping these people undressed, stood around in family groups, kissed each other, said farewells and waited for a sign from another S.S. man, who stood near the pit, also with a whip in his hand.

During the fifteen minutes that I stood near the pit, I heard no complaint or plea for mercy. I watched a family of about 8 persons, a man and woman, both about 50, with their children of about 1, 8, and 10, and two grown-up daughters of about 20 to 24. An old woman with snow-white hair was holding the one-year-old child and singing to it and tickling it. The child was cooing with delight. The couple were holding on with tears in their eyes. The father was holding the hand of a boy of about 10 years old and speaking to him softly; the boy was fighting his tears. The father pointed toward the sky, stroked his head, and seemed to explain something to him. At that moment the S.S. man at the pit shouted something to his comrade. The latter counted off about 20 persons and instructed them to go behind the earth. Among them was the family which I have mentioned.

I well remember a girl, slim and with black hair, who, as she passed close to me, pointed to herself and said, "Twenty-three!" I walked around the mound, and found myself confronted by a tremendous grave. People were closely wedged together and lying on top of each other so that only their heads were visible. Nearly all had blood running over their shoulders from their heads. Some of the people shot were still moving. Some were lifting their arms and turning their heads to show that they were still alive. The pit was already two-thirds full. I estimated that it already contained about a thousand people.

I looked for the man who did the shooting. He was an S.S. man, who sat at the edge of the narrow end of the pit, his feet dangling into the pit. He had a tommy gun on his knees and he was smoking a cigarette. The people, completely naked, went down some steps which were cut in the clay wall of the pit and clambered over the heads of the people lying there, to the place where the S.S. man directed them. They lay down in front of the dead or injured people; some caressed those who were still alive and spoke to them in a low voice. Then I heard a series of shots.

I looked into the pit and saw that the bodies were twitching or the heads lying already motionless on top of the bodies that lay before them. Blood was running from their necks. I was surprised that I was not ordered away, but I saw that there were two or three postmen in uniform nearby. The next batch was approaching already. They went down into the pit, lined themselves up against the previous victims and were shot.

When I walked back, around the mound. I noticed another truckload of people which had just arrived. This time it included sick and infirm people. An old, very thin woman with terribly thin legs was undressed by others who were already naked, while two people held her up. The woman appeared to be paralyzed. The naked people carried the woman around the mound. I left with Moennikes and drove in my car back to Dubno.

On the morning of the next day when I again visited the site, I saw about 30 naked people lying near the pit — about 30 to 50 meters away from it. Some of them were still alive; they looked straight in front of them with a fixed stare and seemed to notice neither the chilliness of the morning nor the workers of my firm who stood around. A girl of about 20 spoke to me and asked me to give her clothes and help her escape. At that moment we heard a fast car approach and I noticed that it was an S.S. detail. I moved away to my site. Then minutes later we heard shots from the vicinity of the pit. The Jews still alive had been ordered to throw the corpses into the pit — then they themselves had to lie down in this to be shot in the neck.[12]

---

[12]Levin, *The Holocaust*, pp. 264–266.

One man who escaped death wrote to warn other Jews about what was happening:

> My very dear friends,
>
>   I did not answer you until now, because I knew nothing very definite about all the things I've been told. Alas, to our great misfortune, we now know everything! I had here at my home an eyewitness who was saved by the grace of heaven.... I found out everything from him. The place where they are exterminated is called Chelmno, near Dabia, and they are buried in the neighboring forest of Lachow. The men are killed in two ways: shooting or gas.... For several days they have been taking thousands of Jews from Lodz and have done the same to them. Don't imagine that all this is written by a madman. Alas, it is the terrible tragic truth.... "Man, rend thy clothing, put on sackcloth with ashes, and go out into the midst of the city, and cry out with a loud and bitter cry." I am so tired that my pen can write no more. Creator of the universe help us![13]

But the man was not believed. His friends could not accept the truth of what some human beings were doing to other human beings.

In Warsaw, on August 12, 1942, an orphanage for Jewish children was "evacuated." The founder and director was Janusz Korczak, a physician, writer, and educator. As a medical doctor he could have remained in the Warsaw Ghetto for some time longer, but he chose to accompany his children on the deportation. An eyewitness describes the scene:

> And so a long line is formed in the front of the orphanage on Slisks Street. A long procession, children, small, tiny, rather precocious, emaciated, weak, shriveled and shrunk. They carry shabby packages, some have school-books, notebooks under their arms. No one is crying.
>
>   Slowly they go down the steps, line up in rows, in perfect order and discipline, as usual. Their little eyes are turned toward the doctor. They are strangely calm; they feel almost well. The doctor is going with them, so what do they have to be afraid of? They are not alone, they are not abandoned.
>
>   Dr. Korczak busies himself with the children with a sober earnestness. He buttons the coat of one child, ties up a package of another, or straightens the cap of a third. Then he wipes off a tear which is rolling down the thin little face of a child.

---

[13]Ibid., p. 306.

Then the procession starts out. It is starting out for a trip from
which — everybody feels it — one never comes back. All these young,
budding lives.... And all this is marching quietly and orderly to the
place of their untimely doom.

The children are calm, but inwardly they must feel it, they must
sense it intuitively. Otherwise how could you explain the deadly se-
riousness on their pale little faces? But they are marching quietly in
orderly rows, calm and earnest, and at the head of them is Janusz
Korczak.[14]

Must we go on? Can we go on? How can we? And yet we must.
Else the next Holocaust may await all of us, the one that will con-
sume the earth.

Who were the people who devised the policies that Christians and others carried out? Adolf Hitler was a baptized Catholic
who claimed to be doing God's work in killing Jews. Paul Joseph
Goebbels, propaganda expert, came from a strict Catholic family
and had his education, in part, funded by the Albertus Magnus
Society. Auschwitz's Commandant Rudolf Hoess said he took his
Catholic religion "very seriously." Heinrich Himmler, the ruthless
head of the SS was from a devout Catholic family. Reinhard Heydrich, who led the Reich Security Service, was Catholic. It has not
gone unremarked that Hitler's heir apparent, Hermann Goering,
was given the full funeral rites of the Lutheran church.

Resistance

We must not leave the impression that these men were followed
blindly by all Europeans, or even that all remained indifferent.
Gordon Zahn has told us the story of Franz Jagersdatter, the Aus-
trian peasant who disobeyed his priest and his bishop and was
martyred for refusing to fight in the German army. Protestant theologian Dietrich Bonhoeffer's resistance and death are also well
documented. And there are, perhaps, several thousand more. The
man who was to be Pope John XXIII, when apostolic delegate to
Turkey, aided Hungarian Jews to escape. The head of the Or-
thodox church in Rumania, Patriarch Nikodemus, courageously
denounced the persecutions and thus no doubt saved the lives of
thousands of Jews. Bulgaria's Metropolitan Stephan insisted that

---

[14]Ibid., p. 326.

God alone could determine the fate of the Jews and that human beings had no authority to persecute them and led resistance in his country. Italians did not cooperate with Hitler's Jewish policies.

A French Capuchin, Fr. Marie-Benoit, helped organize a mill for the creation of false documents, including certificates of baptism, to help Jews escape. Railway workers in Belgium earned honor in aiding Jews on transport trains to escape the crematoria by refusing to lock the railway car doors. Nora Levin reports that "20,000 Dutch Christians were deported to concentration camps because they opposed Nazi racial decrees, many of them first to Buchenwald, where they were slowly tortured, then to Mauthausen in Austria."[15] Of two thousand Jews in Finland, only four were deported. In Galicia, Metropolitan Andreas Szeptycki, Archbishop of Lvov who headed the Ukrainian Greek Catholic church, refused to allow religious service of any kind to Ukrainians who killed Jews. This half-paralyzed, seventy-seven-year old man personally hid Jews in his quarters and ordered nuns in convents to do likewise.

The story of Danish non-cooperation is probably best known around the world. It is said that when Jews in Denmark were ordered to wear the star of David as an emblem of humiliation, King Christian X, followed by the rest of the citizens, did likewise. The tale is not literally true, but it does have symbolic veracity. It seems that nearly all Danes, including their monarch, were extremely supportive of their co-citizens, the Jewish Danes. There were some 7,000 Jews in Denmark, and 474 were caught by the Gestapo and sent to concentration camps. The majority were rescued and spent the remainder of the war years as free persons in neutral Sweden.

The Danes were motivated by an admirable sense of individual responsibility. Jorgan Barford, who was president of the Association of Danish Prisoners from the Fight for Freedom, tells this story:

> The German Plenipotentiary in Denmark, Dr. Werner Best, raised the matter of an action against the Jews with his superiors in Berlin on September 8th, 1943. Best happened to mention this to the German shipping expert in Denmark, G. F. Duckwitz, who was an opponent of the Nazis' terror methods and who had made contact with some Danish Social Democrat politicians, H. Hedtoft-Hansen and H. C. Hansen. Duckwitz was furious and even went to Berlin to prevent this manhunt

---

[15] Ibid., p. 409.

from being put into effect, and later went to Stockholm for the same purpose. However, by the 28th of September he had to admit that he was powerless, and as he by then knew the date when the persecution of the Jews was to begin, he passed on this information to the above-mentioned Danish politicians.[16]

The politicians then warned the head of the Jewish community, High Court Advocate C. B. Henriques, and the message was communicated to nearly every Jew in the country. When the Germans came to arrest Jews, very few were at home, many being given refuge by Christian friends. In 1943 Bishop H. Fuglsang Damgaard wrote a pastoral letter on behalf of all Danish bishops to be read in churches throughout the country. It stated:

The Danish bishops have on September 29th, this year, forwarded the following communication to the leading German authorities through the heads of the government departments:

Wherever Jews are persecuted as such on racial or religious grounds the Christian Church is in duty bound to protest against this action:

1. Because we can never forget that the Lord of the Christian Church, Jesus Christ, was born in Bethlehem of the Virgin Mary according to God's promise to His Chosen People, Israel. The history of the Jewish people before the birth of Jesus contains the preparation for the salvation God has prepared for all mankind in Christ. This is shown by the fact that the Old Testament is a part of our Bible.

2. Because persecution of the Jews conflicts with that recognition and love of man that are a consequence of the gospel which the church of Jesus Christ was founded to preach. Christ is no respecter of persons, and He has taught us to see that every human life is precious in the eyes of God (Gal. 3:28).

3. Because it conflicts with the concept of justice which prevails in the Danish people, settled in our Danish Christian culture for centuries. In consequence of this, equal rights and responsibility before the law, and freedom of religion, are secured to all Danish citizens according to the words of the constitution.

We regard religious freedom as the right to worship God according to vocation and conscience and hence that neither race nor religion can, of themselves, deprive any citizen of rights, liberty or property. Despite differences of religious opinion, we will struggle for the right of our Jewish brothers and sisters to preserve the same liberty that we prize more highly than life itself.

---

[16]*Escape from Nazi Terror* (Copenhagen, 1968), p. 11.

The leaders of the Danish Church are fully aware of our duty to be law-abiding citizens, who do not set themselves up against those exercising authority over us, but at the same time we are in conscience bound to assert the law and to protest against any violation of it. Therefore we shall, if occasion should arise, unequivocally acknowledge the words that we should obey God rather than Man.[17]

The rest is inspiring history. The smuggling of Jews into Sweden took a widely coordinated and extremely secret effort. Many persons risked their freedom and their lives in this defiance of the Nazis. The role of Swedish citizens must also be commended. There was not as much personal risk involved, certainly, but the Swedes didn't merely accept the new immigrants. They trained them in the language, found them jobs and places to live, and did risk infuriating German authorities whose war plans always proved capricious enough so that even neutral Sweden had to be wary.

Nor should the Protestant community of Le Chambon, in France, go unmentioned. There, five thousand Christians, led by their pastor, helped to hide and save five thousand Jews without a single betrayal. These people were all willing to risk their lives *to save strangers*. But such stories are, unhappily, not common.

Nor should we be surprised at this. We only have to ask ourselves, "How would I have acted under such circumstances?" The honest answer might prove shocking. No one can be certain how she or he would act in time of crisis. We each might find many ways to excuse ourselves from risking our safety, risking the security of our families, of not wanting to get involved for one reason or another. News accounts are too common that report how, while crimes are being committed, while a person is being attacked, passersby, even neighbors, look the other way and refuse to lend even token resistance such as a scream or a quiet call to the police. So as we judge the silence of so many, we must not thereby feel smug about what we might do during tragic times.

To Be a Christian ...

Many Christians simply were not very helpful to Jews during the war, even Christians of high ecclesiastic rank. For example, the

---

[17] Barford, *Escape from Nazi Terror*, pp. 12–14.

Vatican was asked by the Vichy government in France about the law of June 2, 1941, which isolated Jews and deprived them of their rights. The response was direct. "In principle, there is nothing in these measures which the Holy See would find to criticize."[18] There is even evidence to lead one to conclude, as Nora Levin has, that early in the war, at least, "the Vatican expressed its interest in a German victory."[19] Later, there were perhaps other reasons for Rome's inaction. "When Dr. Eduardo Senatro, the Berlin correspondent of *L'Osservatore Romano*, asked him whether he would not protest the exterminations, the Pope [Pius XII] is reported to have answered, 'Dear friend, do not forget that millions of Catholics serve in the German armies. Shall I bring them into conflicts of conscience?'"[20]

Unhappily, Pius was not alone in his silence. Even the U.S., with its large Jewish population, did comparatively little. And Great Britain, with Anthony Eden as a great stumbling block to Jewish rescue efforts, almost actively persecuted Jews trying to escape Hitler. No one knew what was happening? Henry Morgenthau, Jr., secretary of treasury in the United States, gives the lie to this:

> We knew in Washington, from August 1942 on, that the Nazis were planning to exterminate all the Jews of Europe. Yet, for nearly 18 months after the first reports of the Nazi horror plan, the State Department did practically nothing. Officials dodged their grim responsibility, procrastinated when concrete rescue schemes were placed before them, and even suppressed information about atrocities in order to prevent an outraged public opinion from forcing their hand.... The Treasury's responsibility for licensing monetary transactions abroad meant that we had to pass on the financial phases of refugee relief plans. This gave us a front-row view of those 18 terrible months of inefficiency, buck-passing, bureaucratic delay and sometimes what appeared to be calculated obstructionism.... Cautious action.... Lacking either the administrative drive or the emotional commitment, they could not bring about prompt United States action on behalf of the desperate people.[21]

So the annihilations went on, with impunity, as it were. Heinrich

---

[18]Fleischner, ed., *Auschwitz: Beginning of a New Era?*, p. 12.

[19]Levin, *The Holocaust*, p. 685.

[20]Ibid., p. 691.

[21]Ibid., p. 669.

Himmler, who insisted that members of the SS must believe in
God, could thus, speak of the honor and decency of the work of
slaughter: "By and large, however, we can say that we have performed this task in love of our people. And we have suffered no
damage from it in our inner self, in our soul, in our character."[22]
And there was no significant challenge. Not even after the terrible events of 1939–1945 was there a moral cry of pain from certain
quarters. Goering was buried with full funeral rites of the Lutheran
church, as noted. Until recently, a mass was celebrated annually in
Madrid for Hitler (though not for the victims) and it has not been
lost on investigators that, at the war's close, the Vatican and others
close to it helped thousands of war criminals to escape, including
Granz Stangl, the commandant of Treblinka. "In 1948, the German Evangelical Conference at Darmstadt, meeting in the country
which had only recently carried out this genocide, proclaimed that
the terrible Jewish suffering in the Holocaust was a divine visi-
tation and a call to the Jews to cease their rejection and ongoing
crucifixion of Christ."[23] As Irving Greenberg has asked, "May one
morally be a Christian after this?" That is the question that haunts
me. Was Christianity in some way buried at Auschwitz? If so, is
a resurrection of a more humanly significant Christianity — less
dedicated to its own preservation and more to the teachings of
Christ, not so fixed on the next world that it is incapable of inter-
acting with this world — is such a resurrection taking place in us,
in me? That is the motivation for my words. What I have written
here only hints at a response. The meaningful answers will come
from lives, not books or talks.

---

[22] Fleischner, ed., *Auschwitz: Beginning of a New Era?*, p. 38.
[23] Ibid., pp. 12–13.

Chapter 3

The Evidence

How does one approach a subject of such moral and emotional magnitude as the atrocity photography of the Holocaust? And yet, once the subject has become visible, how can it be ignored? I want to explore its significance for myself as a professing Christian. I insist that each post-Holocaust Christian must also approach this overwhelming subject if her or his Christianity is to be meaningful. And I want to show survivors of that catastrophe (and that means every person on earth in one way or another) that we Christians are sincere in our examination of what occurred in a Christian — though not a Christ-centered — civilization. The Holocaust is a failure in Christian history. Is Christianity dead? If so, I must know it. If it lives, how is this so, and how is my own religious commitment affected?

Who am I to take up questions of such magnitude? Nobody special. I don't feel that I am doing anything that many others cannot do better. My only response is that I *am* doing research and writing on the Holocaust where enough others are not.

The photographs in this volume were acquired at Yad Vashem Holocaust Memorial Center in Jerusalem. In the archives there are some forty thousand photos of which these few are representative. I had planned to spend three weeks on the project. After two weeks, having gone through about ten thousand photographs, I abruptly left Israel. The research had such an overwhelming impact on me that I had to come home to kiss my wife and hug my children. For this revised edition of this volume, I returned to Yad Vashem several times and completed viewing all of the photos.

Ovens for human beings. Are these the symbol of our century? That someone even thought of them is staggering enough. Many others, of course, had to approve of them: committees, officials, the very highest Nazis. Their designers would have to be approached. "Will you blueprint ovens for us so that we can dispose of Jewish bodies? This will help us free Europe of a pestilence and it will leave no trace of what we did." Could the reply have been, "It will be an honor to serve the Reich"? Next there are the contractors. Was there competitive bidding for the job of constructing these furnaces? Were government officials bribed so that certain companies might gain advantage over others? How much profit was made by the people who helped in this way to carry out the final solution to the Jewish problem?

This photograph is of ovens at Dachau. The three men who are placing the body into the crude crematorium are called *Sonderkommandos*. They are themselves prisoners whose job is to dispose of other prisoners. Usually, a *Sonderkommando* worked about three months at his job, then he himself became a victim of the ovens. This seems to be clearly a public relations photograph of some kind. A special effort is being made here to tell someone something. Otherwise, given all we know of camp efficiency, all of the ovens would have been operating at once. How else could up to nine thousand bodies a day be disposed of? Did the photographer have anything to say to the workers? Did he balance them off for aesthetic purposes? Did he have to make certain that each was so positioned that the body was in no way blocked from view? What are the *Sonderkommandos* thinking as they are being forced to pose? Has their work destroyed their sensibilities? Are they totally beyond caring? Note the lack of other men, the neatness of the area where we might expect grim filth. Public relations photograph indeed.

How old is the bottom figure in this photograph? Perhaps seven. But his eyes contain centuries. What a pitiful incongruity. Innocence, by its very nature, does not encompass experience. But then this photograph is of a situation that is not consistent with nature. The Holocaust was, by every civilized measure, anti-natural. The boy intuits this. Something is horribly topsy-turvy, terribly frightening. A man is holding a weapon on him during this roundup of Jews in Warsaw. For what reason? No reason could ever be invented to justify what is happening in this scene and the real cause is ludicrous in the root sense of that word. This boy is being taken to his death because he has been judged a danger to European equilibrium. He is a Jew. That is crime enough in some people's minds. And while we could focus our attention exclusively on him in this picture, there are others who need to be considered. For instance, the child with his hands raised isn't even the youngest Pole in the group. Just above his right shoulder we see another who is about four or five years old. Another threat, another Christ-killer to some. The boy to the left of center, looking off to his right, also exhibits in his eyes a terror no child should know.

Eyes, in fact, can be considered a theme, if we dare to be academic about this setting. The camera's eye must be considered. It *must* be. Who has dared to take this photograph? For what purpose? Why memorialize this sin? What is the intended audience? Who will enjoy viewing this? The victims were not snapping shutters. No, the persecutors were. Note that no eyes of the prisoners are looking at the camera. Those eyes are concentrated on something other than publicity. There is one, however, who is looking directly into the lens: the guard who has his gun pointed at the little boy up front. We may take it that he is posing for this photographer. Why? Is he proud of what he is doing? Is he pleased to be carrying out his government's policy concerning Jews? Did he request a copy of the photo to show his friends and family? Does he ever wonder if God's eye has recorded the same event? Does he have some thoughts about Judgment Day? What else did he do in the war that is memorable?

What unlimited power individual soldiers had. Almost nothing could stop their outrageous behavior. In fact some wished to record human abuse in order to enjoy it later as the photographer of this snap apparently did. The woman on the left is physically attractive. But she is not proud of her body at the instant recorded here. We can only imagine what comments the soldiers are making about her nakedness. Perhaps the photographer joined in the merriment. It is possible, even likely, that the picture taker is another soldier who joins the others in taking turns at humiliating prisoners. "Next time you take *my* photo," he may have said. And we wonder, "Why the photography?"

The woman's body language is so obvious. Her somewhat stooped shoulders indicate her inward attitude. The set mouth, the downcast eyes all contribute to her personal "atmosphere" if we may say that. What was she before the war? A teacher, a secretary? Perhaps a student. No doubt somebody's sister, a daughter and a granddaughter. A neighbor too, the friend of many and possibly a fiancée. She may even have been married. (There is no ring on her finger but Germans appropriated such things almost immediately.) Did she have children? There is no question that some of the people with whom she had normal human relationships probably saw this moment. The woman on the right, who shared it, may have been her sister or her friend. What happened after the photo was snapped? Did the Nazis touch these women? Did they make them walk the street nude, dance for them, howl like dogs? Nazis did it with others, we know. Were these soldiers braggarts about their contributions to the war efforts of the Third Reich? Did they tell about their heroic behavior on occasions like this?

It is difficult to think of the men looking out through the barbed wire as in any way fortunate, and yet, relatively speaking, they are — because they are near some ventilation on the railroad car into which they have been crammed. If their ride is typical of the experience of so many others, this access to air may save their lives. Other women and men have ridden for days without food or water to their destruction camp. Some experienced 100° heat — others freezing temperatures. Many did not survive. Others went insane. A host saw relatives and friends, babies and the very old, die during the trip.

The majority of these deaths, we learn, were agonizing for those who perished and for the helpless who watched as well. People befouled themselves. Washing facilities were, of course, non-existent. On many of the freight cars sleeping space — that is, room in which to lie down — was also non-existent. Fights broke out among prisoners who, in their frustrations, turned on each other the anger meant for their captors. Corpses on the trains caused disease since some persons died within minutes after having been herded onto the prison on wheels.

Who were the railroad engineers who carried the human cargo to camps of destruction? Who were the laborers who locked tightly the handles on the freight cars (as seen in this photograph) that assured the Nazis that their quarry would arrive at journey's end? (There were Dutch and Belgian railroad workers who saw to it that, when the Nazi troops left after supervising the boarding of the trains, the handles on the freight cars were mysteriously opened again.) And what of the many citizens who watched the cattle cars go by, load after load after load, without pity or protest? We condemn them. But if we were in their positions would we have ... ?

The legend etched in Hebrew beside this heap of human bones says this: "Among the transgressions of the Germans." A pile of broken skeletons, saved from becoming fertilizer by the conquering Allied forces. For some reason the skulls at the lower left have been arranged in an orderly fashion beside the random mass of other bones in this pyramid of infamy. Perhaps the skulls were to be used for some sort of medical experimentation — the kind that we know took place through which the Nazis were trying to prove, by measurements, the inferiority of Jews, Gypsies, and certain others. Or possibly the skulls were so displayed by zealous liberators who wanted to be sure that the full impact of this scene would register in the minds and hearts of us, the viewers. As if we wouldn't be horrified enough without such preparations! How long were prisoners subject to viewing scenes like this one, even while they could hear the guns of British, Russian, or American forces coming ever closer to that long hoped for yet seemingly impossible moment when the barbed wire seen here could be torn down and people could once again resume the tradition of being people?

The legend, "Among the transgressions of the Germans" is so succinct, so telling, so properly understated. Anyone could be practically emotionally destroyed by such atrocities. Do we become immune to them, at some level of saturation? Are we in danger of identifying with one American journalist who immortalized herself on a radio talk show by responding to something another guest had said by saying, "Oh, here we go with those six million again"? She was disgusted that anyone would want to keep remembering the Holocaust, its victims and its implications.

In the emotionally disorienting world of the concentration camp, we cannot be certain that the death of this man was met with sadness by all the prisoners. Some may have stood to gain from his death. Perhaps he left behind a decent pair of boots or a precious spoon. Maybe he had a preferred sleeping place that one of the other men could now acquire. It is possible that this man was in such a weakened condition that another had to work extra hard to cover for him, and so the stronger man would feel relieved when he learned that his burden had been temporarily lightened. Under normal circumstances we would criticize such opportunism as selfish, morally reprehensible.

But we do not here consider normal times. We may dare to suggest that while the letter of certain moral codes was violated, sin among most victims at Auschwitz did not take place. Lying is wrong, but for a twelve-year-old boy to say he is sixteen, so that he might be allowed to live as a laborer rather than perish as a child, is not to sin. Stealing is regarded as a fault, but for a prisoner to smuggle an extra bowl of soup, or a pair of socks off a dead body, is to commit no fault. To fail to love one's neighbor as one's self — when one's neighbor is one's guard, one's captor, one's tormentor — is not to fail morally at all. When we learn that some prisoners killed Nazis, changed sexual preferences, committed suicide — all traditional taboos in our culture — dare we accuse these men and women of anything? What of women or boys who prostituted themselves to survive? How easy it would be to turn on them and point a superior finger. But anyone who would do so would be one who had not undergone similar pressures. And it would be deflecting the aim of where the finger should be pointing — toward the perpetrators of the Holocaust rather than the victims.

How proud can one be of the work one does? Not only so proud as to document it via camera, but also proud enough to use it as the picture side of a postcard. That's right, this snapshot was made into a postcard! That implies that the men in this picture were going to send a lot of messages to a lot of friends, bragging about their contributions to the cause of the Third Reich. Look, pals, here's what we do in the army. There I am, second from the right, doing my part to rid the world of Jews. It is even possible that one or several of the living in this photograph did not participate in the hangings but got into the scene so that they might appear to be "heroes" anyway.

The soldier on the left seems a bit camera shy; his eyes are averted perhaps because he is nervous before the lens. Not nervous because bodies, which he helped to hang, are dangling behind him. Just a little unsure in front of the photographer — like most of us. His smile lets us know what he thinks about his work. Possibly he sent this postcard to his mother. Maybe she would show it with pride to other family members, to neighbors, to friends at the butcher shop.

The facilities for execution here are not the most modern, or even remotely efficient. Thus the victims probably died long, agonizing deaths. Anyone who could grin the way these troops are doing could easily have tormented those about to be murdered; they might readily have enjoyed watching them dangle and gasp for breath. The scene is an isolated one so perhaps no one saw what was going on. The killers had great freedom. On the other hand, since no one could see, why not take a photo, or else they couldn't brag.

All soldiers remember target practice during their days as new recruits in the military. There were all the jokes about someday that bull's-eye turning into the hated enemy. No doubt that enemy was conceived as another soldier, one who posed some threat in return. Danger — there is the vocation of the man in uniform. It is seen as honorable to risk one's life to defend national ideals. How ironic all that rhetoric is when applied to what the rifleman in this photograph is about to do. He is almost a model for marksmanship trainees. True, his right elbow is probably a little lower than most instructors would like, but his left hand grips the weapon properly and his stance, with feet spread apart for good balance, is certainly correct.

Most everything is "right" except the target. An unarmed father, it appears, is shielding his child from the inevitable which is just a few feet from the back of his head. We can imagine the kind of gaping wound that will result from such close-range shooting. We wish to ask this Nazi the questions we want answered by so many others: "How do you justify what you did here?" "How many times did you commit such atrocities?" "Did you welcome such assignments?" (After all, these were the safer duties; far back from the front lines, with unarmed and dispirited victims.)

And the father, what was going on in his mind? Certainly there was no hope for him or the child. Perhaps his only prayer was for swift death for both of them. That is not the kind of prayer that most of us have for our children. It is an unnatural prayer, bred by an unnatural time. No doubt the child had more hope unless the child had seen others gunned down in similar fashion seconds and minutes and hours and days before.

Nobody could accuse the Germans of not having a sense of humor. The entrance to Auschwitz is bridged by the words, "Work makes one free." That's the kind of slogan we might expect in a Charlie Chaplin film where a greedy business mogul is actually trying to enslave his employees in order to increase production. The use of the word "free" in connection with the camp prisoners is scandalously ironic.

Over another camp prisoners who entered read the words, "Homeland of the Jews." This was in mockery of Zionists, whose aspiration was to re-establish Israel (which at that time was not a political entity) so that those Jews who wished might have a country in which they could feel they truly belonged. If by "homeland" is meant not only the place where one finds one's roots but also the site where one dies, then that word was truly used.

More honest, more appropriate words, are now found on a plaque in the infamous camp of Dachau. They are of the American philosopher George Santayana: "Those who forget the past are condemned to repeat it." The wisdom of this statement is what spurs certain people to keep the memory of the Holocaust alive. There is no attempt here to wallow in the inhuman events of that great tragedy. Rather there is the hope (and "hope" is a term not usually associated with the Holocaust) that perhaps, by recalling what happened before and during the Nazi regime, we can prevent similar crimes from occurring.

A Russian proverb puts it even more bluntly than Santayana, and Aleksandr Solzhenitsyn uses it to begin his *Gulag Archipelago*: "Forget the past and you'll lose both your eyes." The past, all of it, is our heritage. Either we learn from it or we do not. Either we shall prepare for new holocausts for our children and grandchildren or we shall not.

Initially one could mistake what is going on in this scene. A group of children, walking in an orderly fashion, to get on some trucks. Perhaps going to a picnic, a zoo outing, a museum visit. That's what children do. But the situation here is grotesquely different. These children are enemies of the Third Reich, the thousand-year empire that Adolf Hitler is constructing. They are Jews, as can be seen by the stars of David on the backs of a number of coats. As Jews, their blood threatens Aryan blood and therefore must commingle only with the earth, not with other blood.

Scholars indicate that of the approximately six million Jews who perished at the will of the Nazis and their collaborators, about a million were under the age of twelve. As we think of the terror, the loneliness, the sense of abandonment, perhaps of betrayal by their parents, that each child experienced, we can feel only shame at what human beings were able to conceive, let alone execute.

One boy seems to be dressed in a sailor suit. When his mother bought it for him, did he put it on proudly, looking forward to the day when he would be in his nation's navy, wearing an official uniform? Many boys have such dreams. What was he thinking about when the photograph was taken — something less pleasant we can be sure.

Four adults can be distinguished in this picture, all grim faced, no doubt because they *know*. The woman at the left of the column has her yellow star displayed. How does she feel as she tries to comfort the youngsters, perhaps telling them soft lies about where they are going, trying not to terrorize them because how can they understand? But how could anyone understand, then or now?

In many of the scenes gathered in this book, faces tell us much of the story. But here they are unnecessary. A woman with four children walking near the railroad tracks that have brought them to an undreamed of destiny captures our thoughts. Are the youngsters hers? The eldest is walking behind since mother has only two arms; she can't wrap her futile protection around all of them. The baby is next to mom, another daughter to their right. The head of a son can be seen just ahead of the woman. He is now the man of the family since, no doubt, the father has been taken from them in one way or another.

Perhaps this is a grandmother, aunt, neighbor, even a stranger who took it upon herself to comfort abandoned children who are terrified because of all that they have seen recently. The children themselves may not have been related, possibly meeting a little while ago as this shepherdess gathered her innocent flock to ease their pain before slaughter. And the photographer, what did he see? Did he have a good eye for composition? Was he satisfied at the tale signified by these human beings slouching toward destruction?

Just an ordinary chimney, rising upward to float its discharge of ashes high above the community in which it is located. But because of chimneys like this at the crematorium at Mauthausen, some Jews regard the clouds in the sky as symbols of dead relatives. We don't know how many bodies were reduced up this chimney, and it is almost blasphemous to speculate. If it had been just one body, that would be horrible. But what if the reality is closer to a quarter of a million? Or many more? The imagination is numbed by this possibility. The age of mass production became the time of mass destruction. The techniques of tremendous efficiency developed by industry were perverted for demonic uses.

Jews have a religious obligation to pray *Kaddish* at the grave sites of their loved ones. Six million dead Jews either have no identifiable graves (countless having been interred in huge burial pits, often crunched in by bulldozers) or have no graves — their ashes were simply scattered from the orifices of giant chimneys that frequently did their work nonstop, day and night, for long periods of time. Some crematoria were capable of disposing of twelve thousand bodies a day. Thus no rabbi or descendant can pray near the remains of these people.

Perhaps it is more accurate to say that the remains of the victims actually are near us all the time. They are practically ubiquitous just as the crimes that destroyed them were all-encompassing in their evil. It may border on sentimentality to think of clouds representing people, or stars symbolizing the eyes of the dead children of the Holocaust. And yet...

Such care is being taken to hang this woman properly. Look at the expressions of each of these men. They are paying such close attention to every last detail. They perform rather artistically for the photographer here, each relating so intently to a particular aspect of the unholy task literally *at hand(s)!* Note how well dressed the men are. The executioner on the left wears trousers that have been carefully creased. (This was long before the invention of perma-press.) And how about the man working from above, with tie and hat. When he left home, did his neighbors think that he was heading for the office? Did he ask his wife, "What's for dinner tonight?" — thinking that today's work would not interfere with a hearty appetite?

But we cannot consider only the killers. Our eyes are continually brought back to the woman who is soon to die. She seems hardly to pose a threat. She looks like my grandmother, is probably somebody's grandmother. What is she thinking? Is she praying? How frightened is this woman? Does she hope for some miracle to save her, or does she despair because she knows that a tremendous human slaughter is taking place, that she is only a single unit in an overwhelming event that will number millions of units?

She may be almost at peace; somehow the camera suggests this. How many has she seen hanged before her? The corpse on the right suggests that there may have been several. How long will she be able to maintain a certain dignity, before she begins to flail her legs and arms in some futile gesture toward life? Did she know the shrouded victim? Was it her husband or a child of hers? Did she die quickly?

A camp orchestra — there's a touch. Many Jewish artists, among them outstanding musicians, would "naturally" be incarcerated if all Jews were arrested. So these talented people could be made to perform. Either that or they would die immediately. Some call that a choice. We learn from Josef Bor in *The Terezin Requiem* and from Fania Fenelon (herself a member of a women's orchestra at Birkenau) in *Playing for Time* that programs were conducted for the entertainment of Adolf Eichmann, Heinrich Himmler and SS officials whenever it was convenient — for the Nazis.

We can only speculate on whether or not the authorities got *extra* pleasure from concerts that were performed by people who had been degraded, had lost everything, were starving, and were subject to massacre. Did Himmler ever regret that a particular outstanding soloist was not going to be thrilling audiences for much longer? Did Eichmann, after enjoying a symphony played by prisoners, ever have doubts about the inferiority, the subhumanity of all Jews? Camp orchestras, we know, were forced to play at occasions when other inmates were entering gas chambers. The impact on the musicians themselves must have been curious. No doubt some thanked their parents for having started them off musically. Perhaps others were horrified because they found themselves hoping that other good players would die off so that the competition — literally for their very lives — would become less intense. What if a so-so cellist learned that a first-rate cellist had just been transferred into the same camp? The newcomer might unwittingly become the enemy of the less accomplished performer. The *real* enemy, the Nazis, may well be overlooked under the incredible conditions. And Nazi music lovers enjoyed!

This is arrival at Auschwitz. Here is both the end of the beginning and the beginning of the end. No men in the photo — the separation of women and children from their males has already taken place. How long these people may have suffered on the train of death we do not know, but the recent history etched in their faces is not to be measured by time but by intensity.

Nearly all are looking directly at the camera, with one exception. The old woman, fourth from the right, faces another direction. Is she disobeying an order? Perhaps she does not hear well. It may be that she is indifferent to what is happening, beyond caring, numb beyond involvement. And the children, what are we to say of them? Shouldn't they be smiling somewhere, playing, eating treats, hugging those they love, being protected by those who love them? They are going to die, because they are Jews.

What is the point of having the signs here translated into English? The message is aimed for worldwide consumption. We hate the Jews, and everyone else should too. Notice that the word "jewish" is not capitalized. Is there a message in that? (The word "German" used also as an adjective *is* capitalized). This isn't to be excused as some kind of picketing — this is intimidation. These youngsters, in terms of chronology but perhaps not of hatred, are stationary and they are wearing *that* uniform. It is expected that no good German, no loyal citizen, will buy here.

Never mind that the store owner may have been a German war hero in Kaiser's army; and never mind that he may have been employing many gentile clerks in his store, clerks whose jobs have immediately become jeopardized by demonstrations like this. What did these employees feel regarding the Nazi campaign? Were they so committed to the rightness of Hitler's cause that they gladly sacrificed their jobs for action against the enemy? Or did they think that things were going a little too far? If some were not in total agreement with the boycott policies, for reasons of personal economics or human rights or whatever, were they too frightened to publicly air their feelings? Did they simply "not want to get involved?"

A close look at the two signs here indicates that they were printed. Nobody prints only two signs. We can be sure that many, many more of these were on show all over Germany. We can only wonder at how the Jews felt when they saw these words displayed. They all knew Jewish history, a history of persecutions suffered, but we know from how they *didn't* react that they had no concept of the magnitude of what awaited them. How could they have — the world would never let such a thing happen.

The sloppy oven area at Majdanek. There is a bent body-moving tool in the immediate foreground. How many Jews, Gypsies, Slavs, Russians, Poles, Latvians, Greeks, and others did that device shove into the crematoria? How many different men operated that tool in their incendiary work? Sometimes the furnaces worked almost beyond capacity so that chimneys were in danger of collapsing. At Auschwitz, near the end of the war, twelve thousand bodies a day were turned to ashes. That must have caused a frantic amount of energy to be spent on such activity.

It took tremendous organization, fantastic coordination, awesome assembly-line techniques to round up prisoners, ship them, kill them, remove the bodies from gas chambers, bring them to the ovens, keep the ovens burning at a constant pitch, put the bodies in, be certain that (for efficiency's sake) immediately upon destruction of corpses the doors could be opened again so that more cadavers could be put in. Time was of the essence. The war was coming to an end. German troop trains were being diverted from the front lines — where reinforcements were so badly needed — so that more Jews could be transported to their deaths.

Joseph Goebbels died confident that, regardless of the outcome of the war, the world would be grateful for the Nazi program of a Final Solution to the universal problem of the Jews. Other Nazi officials uttered similar thoughts. How can we respond to this? Either the deaths of millions of Jews and the countless others in the camps are part of an event so terrifying in history that we are utterly determined that such acts must not happen again and that we each take individual responsibility to fight, truly fight injustices everywhere, or . . . or . . .

An execution in Hungary. The man who is about to die is striking a rather defiant pose. He is not trussed up to a pole, not cringing from the irons that are about to penetrate his body. Whatever he did to call a death sentence upon himself does not appear to make him remorseful or so terrified that he loses his dignity before the ultimate mystery.

The police and town officials gathered to witness this killing present a curious picture. None of them is looking at the victim. This is not true of the people in the left and right windows of the building that we face from our close vantage point. The officer second from the left in the front row is looking away (as is another who is partially shielded from us by the rifles). Out of squeamishness? Shame? Does he recognize an injustice being done? Or is he looking around to make certain that everyone else is observing this example, this lesson being taught them so that these other men will not attempt to act contrary to fascist demands?

The sandbags are not packed particularly high — the riflemen are obviously instructed not to aim for the man's head. That would be messy and additionally be somewhat dangerous with the possibility of ricocheting bullets. And we can see that the weapons indeed are aimed heart high. No doubt the town officials were being forced to witness this event. Only two seem to have bared their heads out of a kind of respect for death that such a gesture implies.

What was going on in the minds of the onlookers? Did they learn to love Big Brother, equating that emotion with fear, or were some vowing to fight the Nazis and their collaborators so that the man about to die would not have stood alone against corruption and human disintegration?

There are some who feel that the Holocaust must be reacted to only with silence. Words would somehow cheapen the event. Those of us who do not agree with this opinion are nevertheless often brought to silence when considering a scene such as this one. We can understand why the most effective Holocaust literature, meaning the autobiography, fiction, and poetry given their impulse by this event, is writing of understatement, of suggestion.

One of the most significant of such works is *Night*, by Elie Wiesel. First published in Yiddish, the volume was over 800 pages long. In its revised form, it comes to less than 120 pages. The author, who in *Night* tells of his experiences at Auschwitz, where he lost his mother and sister and saw his father beaten to death, cut away and cut away at the original manuscript, but says that to the sensitive reader it is all still there.

This is an important concept for us if we are to grapple with the Holocaust on any meaningful level. As an author Wiesel is saying to us, "You try to complete what I present to you." There is a certain trust here (as there is in all great art, as there need be in all human relationships) and we must not betray that trust.

The man holding the child's body in this photo may be attempting the same thing with us. We have only to look, no one need utter a word. Civilization has come to this — the horrors that can be perpetrated are reduced to a scene like this.

Incomprehensible — certainly! But we are obligated to try to come as close as we can to understanding the un-understandable. Of the victims of the Holocaust, perhaps a million were children who had not yet reached their teens. As a human race we have been robbed of their love, their vivacity, their talents, their wisdom, their joy. We are considerably poorer for that. Maybe we didn't deserve them.

Again, the eyes have it, they hint at the depths of the event. They suggest the trauma of separation, of exile, of imprisonment for no crimes at all. Every visible face in this photograph is marked with tragedy. These people are on their way to a concentration camp where the series of shocks they will receive will kill some of them before they can be physically murdered. A view of the camp itself, with the guards, the dogs, the fences and barbed wire, the filthy barracks, and above all the condition of the prisoners already there will provide a severe jolt to the psychological health of every man in this crowd.

The exchange of clothing for prison attire — deliberately assigned so as not to fit (including the shoes used for long marches) in order to increase the sense of humiliation — will provide another shock. The dehumanization process will continue as the men are stripped of their names and given numbers, indelibly tattooed on their arms, reminders that they are not persons, merely integers in the Nazi scheme of world domination. The shaving of the heads, of all bodily hair in fact, is another operation calculated to disorient a human being.

So too are the beatings the prisoners will undergo as well as the remarks of abuse, threat, sexual innuendo, and insult coming from those with the least bit of authority in the camps. (Many of these are criminals and sexual offenders, who were given charge over the Jews, Gypsies, Jehovah's Witnesses, and others arbitrarily incarcerated.) Little pranks by the bathhouse staffers, such as the alternating of all cold or all hot water streams, will also cause confusion among the new prisoners.

For the most part, the only thing they can be grateful for is that they have no mirrors in which to see their own degradation. Many survivors were stunned to see themselves, almost unrecognizable, at the time they were freed by Allied troops.

The word "reification" means the opposite of personification. In personification we give human attributes to nonhuman entities. To call an owl wise or to describe a storm as angry is to personify. But in reification we mentally convert a person into a thing: a runner is labelled a "speeding bullet," an intellectually dense child is referred to as a "block of wood," or the term "toy" is applied to a woman.

The Nazis practiced this concept of reification to near perfection. Jews were regarded not as humans but as animals — and so called "lower" animals at that. This was a very successful ploy, or else how could so many men and women help to destroy so many other men and women?

The elderly woman in this photograph was suffering partly because she was not regarded as a grandmother, as one beloved of God, as the possessor of human dignity. Her pain is engulfing. Is the corpse next to her a beloved sister? No doubt the anguish she feels includes an expression of hunger, perhaps chill, possibly fear of the dog that may be crazed in its own hunger. Certainly she is a women without much hope.

Rubble and corpses in the street are so common that most of the others in this scene are not even looking at her. Only one woman, in the upper left hand corner, in better health and over-all condition, it seems, is staring. What is she thinking?

When you think of train travel, what comes to mind? We complain when a train is late, we get upset when the air conditioning (or heat) is off, we demand comfortable seating and expect rapid movement by the engineer. None of this applied to the Polish women here boarding a freight car in Cracow bound for death. They were packed standing on this winter ride with no possibility of heat. They may have been kept locked this way for several days, to be unloaded at the convenience of their captors.

Sometimes, on such journeys, when the train would slow down near certain depots, free civilians would toss slices of bread into the narrow openings of the cars for the entertainment value of watching starving victims fight over the food. In one such case, a boy beat his own father to death to wrest the crumbs the old man had managed to obtain — and then the boy was killed by others who had witnessed the ghastly event.

We can imagine the hysterical atmosphere of the trip. The riders had just been separated from their families, wrenched from their secure homes, dispossessed of nearly everything they owned, rounded up and kept waiting for who knows how long. They were frightened, abandoned, and absolutely mystified. How many times must they have begun questions with the word "Why?" Answers could not be forthcoming. The Germans claimed to have certain answers, of course. But these satisfied no one, perhaps not even the Germans themselves.

The Holocaust itself is a question of overwhelming magnitude, a nearly ultimate enigma with no possible answer. We can respond to it, but we cannot reason about it. That may be why much modern philosophy has tried to ignore its impact on contemporary thought and attitudes. And yet the question of the Holocaust will be ignored only at peril to the entire human race.

"Hey, Hans, let's have some sport. Bring your camera. We'll get this old Jew to make a fool of himself. It shouldn't be hard since all Jews are fools anyway. You, Jew, get over here. Strip. Immediately!" What were the threats that forced this man into this ignominious posture? How much had he seen that convinced him that to disobey might mean instant death or prolonged torture? There was no appeal from the whim of any camp authority, from the commandant down to the criminals who were assigned as barracks chiefs. What is the enjoyment factor in ridiculing another human? Is physical superiority ever a basis for moral superiority?

So many of the persecutors of the Jews called themselves Christians yet the Christ they claimed to follow never glorified force. Who is the finer human being, the city slicker who sells the country bumpkin the Brooklyn Bridge or the naive, trusting buyer who is willing to believe? Who is the finer human being, the guard who is tormenting the man here pictured or the man himself whose eyes, whose entire body, indicate some of the pain he is experiencing? The subject of mockery appears to be standing above floor level, perhaps atop some steps; this will serve as a makeshift stage for an audience of amused guards. Possibly other prisoners were forced to watch as well. Maybe this was part of a circus with a number of inmates forced into the big circle of attention. Did some resist, refuse? What happened to them? We can guess.

Such entertainment had to come after 12–16 hour working shifts when the prisoners were exhausted and needed to rest. Slow or swift deaths were never enough for some of the Nazi authorities and their many collaborators. Kill them, yes, but take away their dignity first. To a devout Jew the privacy of the individual's body is beyond question. Michelangelo's angels were covered by protectors of the public's morality, but at Auschwitz, photographers acted differently with human beings.

Was the photographer pleased with this photograph? We can imagine the apprehension of the picture taker, after having run camera-rampant through Dachau. Maybe he went home and said to his wife, "I hope these pictures from Dachau come out. I got some real good ones today. They'll be very interesting if the developer doesn't mess them up." And when the final product was seen, did the photographer take pleasure in his achievement? Certainly this is not a great picture, but there is a kind of symmetry, a clear balance of line shown here with the upright cremators, the diagonal body, and building lines perpendicular to each other.

We can see that this photograph is posed. The man on the right has his legs so positioned that he obviously is not walking. Possibly the cameraman asked them to stop in their tracks because his talented eye could recognize a dramatic shot when he saw one. What of the two men who are hauling the body? He on the right seems unwilling to cooperate with the photographer other than to halt when ordered — probably by a guard. The other man looks at the lens, but what is he thinking? Is he revenge minded, humiliated, angry, sad, or just another victim? It is not easy to tell from this shot.

And the dead man himself? The bones tell a portion of his suffering, but of course only a portion. He was nearly (if not totally) starved. But what of the humiliation he experienced while alive? What family tragedies did he witness before he himself became one? This man will be incinerated. He will have no burial place, there will be no grave over which some survivors may pray the *Kaddish*.

Bodies piled upon bodies piled upon bodies. How ever was anyone able to adjust to such sights? How could those soldiers who
manned the machine guns light up cigarettes during their fifteen-
minute breaks from murder? How did the men who operated the
bulldozers that swept mounds of corpses into pits for mass burial
escape nightmares each time they went to sleep — and "daymares"
too? Why is it that we repeatedly hear of the suicides of survivors
but we almost never hear of the persecutors committing acts of
self-destruction (unless when captured and brought to trial)?

But there is another direction toward which questions may be
aimed — not questions meant to blame or condemn, but ones that
trouble survivors themselves as well as the rest of us. For example:
How is it possible for prisoners at Auschwitz or Dachau or Buchenwald to keep on functioning in the face of all of the brutality they
see and they suffer? How, when on a march to work, and when
your neighbor beside you drops from exhaustion and is immediately shot by an impatient guard, do you keep on marching as if it
were almost an ordinary thing to do?

We can imagine the conversations taking place in the barracks
at night — no, we don't have to imagine them, because survivors
have told us of the talk that went on at the end of a work day.
"Who died today?" "How many did we lose on the road?" "When
they beat Max, did he die or is he still alive?" Almost matter-of-fact
inquiries that today horrify the survivors themselves who consider
to what they had been reduced. And yet they went on, and they
did survive, and we can bless them for that. As Terrence Des Pres
has noted, for too long we have only glorified the dead as heroes
and we must recognize those who endured the Holocaust as true
heroes as well.

What were the last thoughts of these three people? Were the children so terrified that they clung to their mother in a desperation that only emphasized her helplessness? Or had they experienced so much terror, dislocation, hunger, sickness, that they were beyond thinking that their parents, who had failed them so often these past days, could do anything to help? And the young mother, did she die first or have the additional agony of seeing her babies murdered? Did she call on God in her last moments or was her despair too great? How long did she suffer? How long did she see her children suffer?

The faces of each of these corpses is haunting, crushing. How can the world have gotten so out of control that some of us could do this and be praised by still others for having done so? How can some of our contemporaries claim dissatisfaction because the plan to rid the world of Jews was not completed?

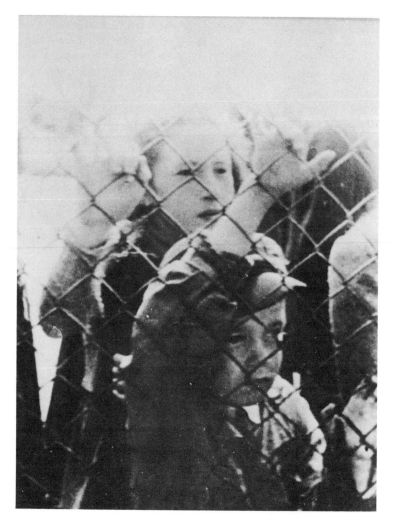

We hesitate to identify the pair in this photograph as children. Chronologically they are — perhaps five and ten years old. But experientially they are old, far older than perhaps anyone ever ought to be. They are living through their own suffering and they are the inheritors of the suffering of their people. This is a centuries-old persecution and it has registered in the sadness of their eyes. We like to see our young smiling and full of hope.

There is none of that found here, but rather defeat, resignation. There is not even a trace of the question "Why?" in this scene. The boy and this girl are beyond framing questions in their minds. Instead they appear to be observers. Theirs is a "What next?" attitude. They have already been taken away from their homes, their comfortable and comforting bedrooms, their neighborhoods, friends, schools, parents, grandparents. Possibly they saw some of their loved ones beaten, murdered. Certainly they saw their authority figures (fathers and mothers, rabbis, teachers) disenfranchised in one swift stroke. All sense of security must have vanished for them in an instant. How did they take it?

How did they adjust? In part, they must have been numbed. Look at their faces. What are these two old children seeing? What has brought a crowd to the fence? Our imaginations may run riot and yet they might not approach the true reality. We know this from eyewitness accounts of what took place during the roundup of the Jews. The crimes of these two children? They are enemies of the Third Reich. They are marked for destruction.

Dare we attempt to provide a biography for this incinerated corpse? Christians did that sort of thing concerning the early martyrs of their faith. The bones of a young child were found in the Roman catacombs, and as a tradition grew about them, she was given a name Philomena and eventually was revered by some as St. Philomena. Biographies were written about her. Recently these life stories were found to be without substance and the Vatican so pronounced. Yet such "poetic" biographies are not hard to construct. We know something about the lives of young Roman girls, about early Christians, about existence in the catacombs. An authentic "novel" could then be built around such a character.

We might do the same for this victim. We know enough to make a convincing plot on just a few facts. If we can ascertain this person's sex, nationality, and approximate age, we might be able to synthesize a life story. No doubt, like most Holocaust victims, this person would have led a rather ordinary life until the Nazi program gained momentum. But then the term "ordinary" was stripped of any possible application to the experience that this woman or man was subject to.

And for us, looking on in anguished wonder, this person takes on a kind of meaning with which no one ought to be burdened. This is indeed a troubling photograph. We may feel troubled not only when contemplating the corpse, but also in thinking about the living Red Cross man. This scene appears to have been posed for the cameraman. We are justified in wondering why. Does the onlooker have a function? Is he there to register an emotion for us that a propagandist wants to be certain that we somehow achieve? Does someone worry that we will not know how to react? Is somebody afraid that we will become numbed too easily?

We have no information about this photograph. Yet we can be certain that it was not taken at the end of World War II, at liberation time. The reason for our certainty is simple: no such large number of old women could have survived any Nazi camp. Since they were not productive workers, and were thus an economic drag, they had to be fed (however meager the rations were), housed, guarded . . . yes, guarded. These grandmothers were forcibly retired into the ultimate old age homes of Dachau, Auschwitz, Treblinka.

For those of us who are increasingly restless in the company of our aging parents, Hitler and Eichmann and Himmler and Hoess have suggested a solution. Kill them. If this sounds obscene, we need only remember that the world stood by, virtually in disbelief, later in absolutely guilty inaction, while these grandmothers were being gassed, starved, shot, burned, or buried alive.

We can also guess from the clothing the women are wearing that they have just recently been taken prisoner. Their garb is not in tatters; they appear to have enough to keep relatively warm (although the woman on the left, closest to the camera, might not agree). But the stunning aspect of this scene is the age of most of the prisoners. No doubt most of these women have earned a right to a comparatively easy old age.

Imagine your grandmother in such a camp, forced to endure long roll calls while standing out in the cold, subject to bodily searches. Could she negotiate the trip each night to the top row of bunks. Could she manage to crawl down safely in the dark to go to the bathroom? Would she have any desire to go on living when separated from the rest of her family, not knowing if her kin are alive or dead? The expression on the face of the woman on the right, near the camera, may answer all of these questions.

Hip deep in bodies: that's what these reluctant prisoners are. Well, *somebody* has to stack them. Indeed they are stacked, not indiscriminately strewn around the railroad car. This orderly arrangement allows for maximum utilization of space. Therefore, time is saved, energy is conserved. This is good for the Nazi war effort. Fewer trips by train will have to be made.

How did these two men first take to their job? We can picture various work assignments given to prisoners, and this pair got this task. Actually, it tells us a little about them. For one thing, we know that they are reasonably healthy, reasonably strong, or else they would not have been selected for this work. From this we may further conclude that they are probably fairly new prisoners, since almost none who were in the camps for any length of time remained somewhat healthy and somewhat strong.

So how did they react to this job? How did they talk about it between themselves? With others? In order to cope, psychologically, did they have to resort to a grim humor to keep from collapsing in despair?

Did they have to block out seeing these corpses as the bodies of human beings and simply treat each one as an inanimate unit of cargo like a brick or board or slab of meat? Did they have the experience of being brought up short in their work, as others in their position were, because they recognized one of the corpses as that of a dead brother or grandfather? (This happened so many times.) Or did they come across mangled, emaciated corpses, unidentifiable, that reminded them of loved ones, that put doubts into their minds as to whether or not these were members of their families? Perhaps one of these men felt that he thus encountered his own father ten thousand times.

"Efficiency" is a key word in the Nazi vocabulary. Nothing must be wasted. Hence all Jewish property was expropriated by the Nazis in the territories that they occupied. When they got their prisoners to camp, they were shorn of all bodily hair. Literally mountains of human hair were collected and transformed into rugs and other items to warm the conquerors. The grizzly topic of soap made from human flesh can never be forgotten in this context. (We do not mention decorations made from human skin, such as lampshades, because such actions were taken more for entertainment rather than efficiency's sake.) Then too there were the medical experiments, a hideous lot of them, that were performed on the bodies of persons who "were going to die anyway."

So we are not surprised, then, at collections of eyeglasses or of artificial limbs taken from the myriads of people who will no longer be able to use them. It was the job of some prisoners, remember, to extract gold from the teeth of the dead. The Nazis were experts at recycling nearly everything.

Only human beings were disregarded. As the war effort became more demanding it was determined that bullets were too expensive to be wasted on killing the millions of Jews and the millions of others — even at the rate of one bullet per victim. Zyklon B, a cheap gas, was put forth by some proud chemist as an efficient answer to the wasteful problem.

Others helped the war effort in an even more severely economic mode, by burying prisoners alive, or burying them without their having first died. People tumbled all over themselves with such suggestions, which were highly appreciated. Such people can't even hide behind the excuse that "I was just following orders."

This photograph was taken at the time of liberation. The man on the ground has just learned that he will not be on the first transport of prisoners going to an Allied army hospital. He seems devastated by the news. This scene is a reminder of the suffering that all survivors of the Holocaust will experience all the rest of their lives, even though they dwell in comparative freedom. Some survivors will never be able to bring themselves to ride on a train again. Many will be pained at merely hearing the German language spoken.

Often, we are told by the survivors themselves and by psychiatrists working with some of them, people experience feelings of guilt for having lived while so many others were unable to. There is a complex variety of reasons for these guilt feelings, but survivors will tell you that so many good people perished and "through some stroke of luck I did not." We should not wonder at the vehemence of their reaction when they hear that the American Nazi Party is planning a march in their community or their refusal to laugh at Holocaust jokes.

Suicides among survivors are abnormally high — but the word "abnormal" applies to so much of their existence. Even their children, as an ever growing body of testimony indicates, have become victims in a way and their lives have been scarred by the experiences of their parents, whom they know, and their grandparents, aunts, uncles, and other family members whom they can only envision as ashes. Family reunions are not very large among the families of survivors. No one has yet done a study on the suicides of survivors, but we cannot help wondering if we have failed them in serious ways.

What does the G.I. think as he looks down in the grave at dead babies after liberation at Nordhausen? There was no liberation for these children, unless death itself may be seen so. But it is blasphemous for those of us who live to see the deaths of others in such a "positive" way. A Christian minister was heard to say, thirty years after Auschwitz, that theologically speaking, the six million Jews are better off dead than alive. Why not kill people right after they are baptized, when their souls are in the purest state they can ever be, according to such a theology!

Another Christian minister, at a convention of editors in the religious press, argued for over three hours (while imbibing scotches in a plush hotel hospitality room) why we had to slaughter the Indians to bring them to Christ. Better known is the remark of the U.S. general who explained the annihilation of a Vietnamese village as an act to save the inhabitants from Communism.

The Nazis, we know, wanted to save the world from something too — from Jews and their nonexistent conspiracy to control the whole world. Something about Jewish *blood* was so threatening that no attempt would ever be made to save boys and girls for a massive re-education program into "Aryan thought." Instead, even they were subject to death by murder. Eyewitnesses tell us not only of babies being starved, and shot (used as targets on some occasions), and gassed, and burned, and buried alive, but of babies being thrown in the air to come down on the points of bayonets, of having their heads bashed against the walls or the ground, of being tossed to killer dogs.

These are truly equilibrium destroying facts. All of us are different because "ordinary" people like ourselves were able to perform such atrocities — or be silent while they happened.

This was a face. It is grotesque, reminding us of novelist Flannery O'Connor's reply to a question about the bizarre situations and characters she rendered to present her theological viewpoint. She insisted that to the hard of hearing you have to shout. The photograph here is a response to those who would hail war as a noble effort, or worse, who would deny that the Holocaust ever really happened. Since over forty books in Europe and the United States have been published denying the actuality of Nazi tortures, let the authors study this picture.

This man was beaten to death with a hammer. Who was he? When he was nursing in his mother's arms, what hopes did she have for him when he reached maturity? Did she dream that he would become a medical doctor who might perform heroic acts of healing? Perhaps she hoped that her baby would become a rabbi and attend the spirit rather than the body. Possibly the boy would be trained as a scientist, become a good family man. He may have been a father. It is not impossible that a son of his saw him being bludgeoned to death. Surely the mother could not have dared to imagine her son's cruel end; he has become, for the world, only a victim, his face and head bones crushed because some guard was somehow irritated with him.

And what of the guard? Was he mad or sane in the way the world ordinarily judges? When he finished his human massacre, was he able to look upon his effort or did it disgust him? Did he brag about his heroics or was he as ashamed of himself as we are of him now? This was a face, the face of a man who lived, and dreamed and died a ghastly death. We cannot look at this face — and yet we dare not avert our eyes lest . . .

The only way out of the suffering for most Jews during the Holocaust was through death. Millions upon millions perished at the hands of those who unilaterally chose the side of the foe. Some victims, however, in their despair, terminated their own lives.

Theorizing about the morality of suicides becomes nearly blasphemous in the face of the desperation of the inmates at Auschwitz, Buchenwald, Dachau, Treblinka and the other institutions of physical and personal annihilations. Moral standards are, after all, meant to apply to normal life situations. While we may cavil about certain dilemmas that women and men are plunged into during the course of earthly existence, it is impossible to categorize the Holocaust events as anything but abnormal — subnormal.

It may not be too strong a judgment to say that the Ten Commandments did not apply to the victims at Auschwitz. Jews and other prisoners were constantly brutalized, were literally treated as things by sadistic guards in a system created specifically for such behavior. People were hungry, ill, dislocated, despairing over the loss of loved ones and home, frightened, exhausted, covered with their own feces and often with filth of those who slept above them on bunk beds. We can have a slight idea of the conditions when we remember that psychiatrist Viktor Frankl refused to wake up fellow inmates who were having nightmares because he felt that the reality to which he would be bringing the dreamer back was worse than the sleeping mind could conjure.

The man in this photograph had to deliberately transverse a warning zone to voluntarily throw his body onto electrically charged barbed wire. A number of inmates sought release this way. Equally depressing is the knowledge that a significant number of survivors of the Holocaust have committed suicide.

The scowl and clenched fists of the man front left of this snapshot are a tribute to the human spirit. We may not be as free as we would like to be in our actions, but we *are* free in our ability to respond to what is happening to us. This man's response to his humiliation is clear and unmistakable.

Like millions of others, these men pictured here were forced to endure roll call. They were often made to stand naked for hours in the most inclement weather. If they fell from exhaustion — and why wouldn't many of them, looking at their shrinking bodies — they were shot. Their guards might beat and otherwise torture them just for amusement. The collar bone of the short man protrudes in a sickening manner; his shoulder angle makes it appear that he may have been seriously injured and must stand awkwardly.

There are true stories of prisoners who survived the Nazi camps who were several inches shorter than when they entered the barracks. One such man had his back broken by a Nazi soldier's rifle butt, and the prisoner kept on working immediately because he knew that if he showed incapacitation he was doomed. Look at the ground on which these men were forced to stand. Not very comfortable. Nothing in their lives in the camps ever was. Maybe this is just a snapshot by a Nazi soldier who wanted to have a memento of his authority?

We can be sure that the men were ordered not to try to hide their nakedness with their hands. And naked indeed they were. All bodily hair has been removed. This had the double effect of obtaining "raw material" to aid the German war effort and to further humiliate prisoners. Note that the two men whose chests are visible on the right have had their identification numbers tattooed onto their chests.

This man did not choose to live in filth. There is very little in his life, at the moment of this photo, over which he has any choice. Ensnared in a ghetto, what would his thoughts be if the question of free will were raised? How easily we talk about controlling our own destinies. Just how much direction can this man give to his existence?

Here he is alone. Was he always so? He has a few possessions. Where are the rest? When was the last time he washed? Laughed? Ate? Was warm? Made love? Enjoyed someone's company? Wasn't afraid? Slept without nightmare? Was free from pain? Felt pride? Had hope? Sang? Prayed? Read? Listened to music? Entered a temple? Danced? All common activities, all things we take for granted. It was decreed that this man, as with so many others, would never again experience the simple rights and pleasures of normal life. And someone decided to immortalize his crisis with a camera.

Many Jews asked where God was at the time of the World War II persecutions. This man, perhaps a rabbi, is forced to carry his symbol of God like an albatross around his neck. Both he and his religion are being ridiculed. In some concentration camps, Jews, who have a long and honorable tradition of dialoguing and even of disputing with God, put the Creator of the universe on trial. Their verdicts varied. In some instances, God was found guilty of having broken his covenant, his agreement, his promise to his chosen people. In at least one case an opposite conclusion was reached. Those sitting in on the judgment, having heard and deliberated on, and prayed over the evidence, concluded that what Jews were undergoing collectively were the birth pangs of the coming of the Messiah, the long awaited Savior of the world long in need of salvation.

Those of us who are not Jewish have another question: Where was Christ at Auschwitz? The death camps rose in the midst of a Christian civilization. How could this have happened? Where was Christian witness, except on a small, ineffectual scale? Where were the official churches? Why were so many silent? Why were so many cooperative? And after the question of Christ at Auschwitz, another has been posed. Where was humankind? Indeed, where was humanity when inhumanity ruled in Europe?

In fact, where is humanity now, after the Holocaust? Have we learned enough from the horrors of that time? Or are Biafra, Indonesia, the Central African Empire, Paraguay, Vietnam, Brazil, El Salvador, Uganda, Cambodia, Iran, Hungary, Lebanon, Ireland, China all evidence that the spirit that endowed the Holocaust lives yet? Are we willing to passively accept this as our nature, or will we work to resist evil in its many forms? If we do not, then all of us will be able to do no more than wear our gods like albatrosses on our own breasts.

These boys ought to be posing for a picture at summer camp. They are of an age where they should be carefree, laughing, unconcerned with the travail of the world. Instead they are forced to stand for a photograph at another kind of camp, one that is the gruesome antithesis of the locations we strive to send our children to. There are no smiles on these faces; there is no hint of merriment in the eyes — old before their time. At a period when young bodies must have proper nourishment for growth and future benefits, these youngsters are being fed on a cup of weak soup daily. Any child who stole a second cup was subject to death.

Elie Wiesel has written of a boy who was caught doing just that. All the prisoners were called out to witness the hanging. The victim's body was so emaciated, so light, that it could not aid him to die quickly at the end of the rope. He struggled with life for over a half hour before he expired. In his memoir, *Night*, Wiesel wrote that after that, the soup tasted of corpses to him.

The agonizing death happened to a child much like the four pictured here. No doubt these youngsters were incarcerated in reasonably good health. Perhaps one or two of them was even overweight. But now we only have to look at their legs, their knees, their ribs, to know of the kind of diet they had suffered over a period of time. Besides malnutrition, such boys and girls experienced many other diseases. The only way for some of them to earn livable rations was to become the sexual favorite of a camp pervert who had some authority. This didn't guarantee longevity, merely a little fuller stomach.

Children of this age need the love, protection, wisdom, security of their parents and it was denied to them. How did they feel about their parents during the crisis? Did the boys and girls feel betrayed, abandoned? Or did they somehow have some understanding of the incomprehensible?

Of over 140 prison and death camps erected under Nazi rule, only
18 were in Germany. Poland hosted 48. Lest we forget where
these camps flourished — *flourished!* — here is a listing.

Austria Ebensee, Gusen, Mauthausen

Belgium Breendonck, Malines

Bulgaria Somovit

Czechoslovakia Novaky, Patronka, Petrzalka, Terezin, Zilina

Estonia Aigali, Ereda, Goldfield, Kalevi, Klooga, Lagedi, Liiva, Vaivara

France Agde, Argeles-sur-mer, Barcares, Beaune la Rodande, Camp du Richard, Compiegne, Drancy, Fort-Barraux, Gurs, Les Milles, Natzweiler-Struthof, Nexon, Pithiviers, Saint-Cyprien

Galicia Borislav, Buchach, Lvov, Plaszow

Germany Arbeitsdorf, Bergen-Belsen, Bochum, Brunswick, Buchenwald, Cottbus, Dachau, Dora, Esterwegen, Flossenburg, Grossrosen, Lichtenburg, Nevengamme, Niederhagen, Oranienburg, Ravensbruck, Sachsenhausen, Wells

Greece Haidon

Hungary Kistarcsa

Italy Bolzano, Fossoli, Mantua, Raab

Latvia Kaiserwald, Salaspils

Libya Giado, Homs

Lichtenburg Lichtenburg

Netherlands Amersfoort, Vught, Westerbork

Poland Auschwitz, Belzec, Belzyce, Birkenau, Bogusze, Bronna Gora, Budzyn, Burggrabben, Chelmno, Chodosy, Chryzanow, Ciezanow, Elbing, Gerdaven, Heiligenbeil, Jaktorow, Jesau, Karczew, Kelbasin, Kielce, Kosaki, Lackie Wielkie, Majdanek, Miedzyrzec Podalski, Mielec, Mlyniewo, Nisko, Peikinia, Plew, Pomiechowek, Praust, Radomsko, Sasov, Schippenbeil, Seerapen, Skarzysko-Kamienna, Sobibor, Stolp, Stutthof, Thorn, Treblinka, Tyszowce, Zaglebia, Zaprudy, Zaslaw, Zawarnice, Zbanzyn

Rumania Caracal, Markulesci

Russia Akmechetka, Bogdanovka, Bratslav, Domanevka, Golta, Kamenka-Bugskaya, Koldychevo, Maly Trostinek, Odessa, Paczara, Sekiryani, Targu-Jiu, Tiraspol, Vapnyarka, Volkoysk, Yedintsy, Zborov

Yugoslavia Ada, Djakova, Jadovna, Jasenovac, Loborgrad, Saymishte

Here we see Hitler youth supervising the humiliation of Viennese Jews. Nazi psychology was profound in many ways. Indoctrinate the young very early. Teach them whom to hate and what to do about it. They heard the Nazi chant, "Germany wake up, Judah drop dead" and the famous battle cry, "Hep! Hep! Hep! Death and destruction to all the Jews."

Hitler himself told the world in his bestselling book, *Mein Kampf* (which was so successful that it made him an independently wealthy man — let us reflect on that!), that people could be made to believe anything if they were told to in the "right" way. It was he who observed in this volume, written during the eight months that he spent in prison for his part in the famed Munich Beer-Hall *Putsch*, that the bigger the lie, the easier it will be for the public to swallow.

And if one lie, why not others? Thus the Nazis were able to effectively use the Jews as scapegoats: It was they who caused the downfall of Germany in World War I; it was they who, as a part of a worldwide conspiracy, helped to keep Germany economically depressed; it was they who tainted the sacred Aryan blood with their own impurities, and hence Jewry had to be extinguished. Fanatics came to believe that Adolf Hitler was the third person of the Christian Trinity: Hitler was called by some the Holy Ghost. The next step is a simple one: if one of the members of the triune Godhead indicated that Jews are God's enemies, then the true faithful are merely doing holy work when they kill the Jews.

And of course starting the "believers" young will help assure success. Notice the number of children in this photograph who are involved in the goings on by way of holding hands to keep the crowd from overflowing into the arena of humiliation. How clever for someone to have arranged for the youngsters to get a closeup view.

Medical experiments, conducted by doctors who had taken oaths not to misuse the knowledge that they had acquired at universities, were performed with tragic frequency. These traitors to humanity conducted experiments to see if typhus could be controlled, to find out if the human system could somehow absorb sea-water, to determine how bodies react to high altitude and to extremely low temperature. The effects of jaundice, injected from infected animals into human systems, were tested. Other experiments included mass sterilization, studying the effects of mustard gas, and the examination of Jewish skulls for traces of racial inferiority.

One of the more hideous of a host of hideous laboratory investigations had to do with the transplant of human bones that were taken from Polish women in Ravensbruck. The doctor who lectured, with pride, to an audience of doctors on his work, was not challenged by any in that gathering. Operations were inflicted on Gypsies to try to prove their blood is different from German blood.

We cannot fail to insist that these monstrous acts were conceived by doctors, approved by other doctors, and carried out by still other doctors, many of whom were decorated for their services to what was to become the Thousand Year Reich. The isolated suffering that many of the victims underwent is symbolized by this photograph. What must it be like to die alone while being tortured? Can anyone maintain hope for self or the universe under such conditions? Or does one even have such thoughts at a time like that? Perhaps the physical pain is so overwhelming that a man or woman can only give attention to that pain.

And the many, many experimenters — how did they feel? Were some euphoric in such assignments, happy to be serving Adolf Hitler, confident in the knowledge that their supply of human guinea pigs was practically endless?

We hear dialogue in gangster movies where the bad guy threatens to blow somebody's head off. The audience never treats that kind of talk seriously and on occasion it can bring snickers from the viewers. The reality, as we see in this scene, is nothing to be laughed at. It is sickening, sickening. All of us, at times, contemplate our own deaths. Teenagers will ask each other, "How would you rather die, by drowning, being shot, or hanged?" Few of us could envision ending up like the man in the center of this photograph, with his forehead ripped off by a machine gun bullet. Death may have been mercifully instantaneous to him while being horrendous and ugly to us, the viewers.

These murdered men are being humiliated, the killers believe, even in death. Their sex organs are exposed as if, somehow, the victims can be demeaned even more. What has happened, instead, is that all humanity is demeaned by both the killings and the exposures of the bodies. We are all less because these things have happened.

If we think about the lives of the three men here, we wonder about their hopes for the future; what did they enjoy in life; how much trouble did they cause? Were they normal, everyday kind of men? Perhaps they were, in life but not in death. Even though deaths like each of theirs were to be shared by millions of other children, women, and men, each death was unique too. All deaths are unique.

But the photograph here evokes a kind of terror in us not only because of the intrinsic horror of the scene but also because of our inability to gain any understanding of what happened. Within the contexts of the various philosophies and theologies extant, the Holocaust is meaningless. We have no framework for comprehending the awe-ful event. How is it permitted that this helpless man's head was blown off? How is it that some *one* could actually commit such an act?

As we contemplate this scene, we might consider the story of Dr. Yaffa Eliach, who tells about her experience as a child survivor of a death camp. Liberation came for her when she was eleven or twelve years old. She emigrated from Europe to Palestine. Not long after arriving in that British governed territory, she accompanied her parents to a funeral. She remembers having asked two questions of her father. "Where are the other bodies?" and "Who killed this person?"

At the threshold of teenagedom, little Yaffa Eliach did not know that people died one at a time and she did not know that people could die natural deaths. Her own life experience did not lead her to know anything else. With scenes like the one shown here vivid in her mind, we can understand how this would be so in her life. The shape of the ongoing psychological tragedy of the Holocaust, for the survivors, is so grotesquely different from anything that most of us have ever known about that we are stunned to learn of the scope and magnitude of the torment.

There is a woman who has a mother and father who married after the Holocaust. Previous to World War II, each of her parents have been married to other partners and each had children. This woman's parents each lost an entire family. After the war, they met and were married. This woman feels immense guilt when she considers the fact that were it not for the Holocaust, she might not have been born. To put it so very bluntly, had her father's first wife and her mother's first husband not ended up on a heap of bodies similar to the one shown here, she might not be alive to carry the burden of her existence.

Indeed the psychological effects of the great atrocity are so incomprehensible in the main that psychiatric assistance to the victims, both survivors and the children of survivors, is limited at best.

Yes, his feet are off the ground. And "yes" answers the question we each have about his shoulders too. There is nothing this man can do to alleviate in any manner the pain he is experiencing on this torture post at Dachau. How long he must hang we do not know. Sixty seconds would be excruciating and these punishments were often handed out for eight hour periods. Any kind of movement will increase this man's torment. If he faints, chances are that some guard will revive him so that he might not escape the feeling of punishment.

And what might have been the "crime" for which this man is being punished? Did the shape of his nose offend someone? Possibly he complained about an aspect of camp life. Maybe, when someone else was being tortured and the prisoners were forced to witness the victim being made an example of, this man averted his eyes out of compassion, shame, disgust, fear. Perhaps he stole a second cup of soup when one cup was meant to suffice for the entire day. At a certain point during this meat-hooking, this human being undoubtedly lost control of his bodily functions.

We probably can't even imagine the condition he was in, if he survived this treatment. His arms would be almost functionless. He could not clean or feed himself for a very long time. Since he would not be able to work, and the authorities were unwilling to "carry" those people who did not earn their keep — that would be bad economics — this man's chances for living much beyond the time he is seen in this picture are minimal.

Did he know that he was photographed here? Did the photographer try to remain unobtrusive or did he tease the victim? "Hey, Jew, look up, smile." Many people participated in the torture and death of many people.

Badly beaten people like this one at Lodz were commonly seen in the camps. In the thirteenth century, St. Thomas Aquinas wrote that we cannot love what we do not know. But today we ask, "How can we hate persons whom we do not know?"

Chaim Kaplan, one who did not outlive the Holocaust but whose *Scroll of Agony* did, posed this very question. "After all," Kaplan noted of one of the many terrifying incidents, "the victim was a stranger, not an old enemy; he did not speak rudely to him (the aggressor), let alone touch him. Then why his cruel wrath! How is it possible to attack a stranger to me, a man of flesh and blood like myself, to wound him and trample upon him, and cover his body with sores, bruises, and welts, without any reason?"

What could this woman shown here have done to warrant such a beating? How offensive could she have been to someone who was physically more powerful than she? Possibly she was merely trying to defend a friend, a relative, a child of hers from harm. If so, she was acting normally; but her treatment in return was far from normal. The blood-clotted face is almost like a map of persecution. The woman's obviously beautiful hair, flowing behind her, no doubt was used as a frame to highlight what was perhaps a quite lovely face. She was no doubt the pride of some man in her appearance; she may have made a number of men's hearts pound a little differently than usual when she walked by because of her physical charm.

But now she cannot be concerned with her appearance. We can guess that only pain and survival are matters for attention. Is she aware that she is now being photographed? If she is, then she must also know the reason she is the object of interest; not because she is lovely to look at but rather because she looks horrible. She is right at this instant reduced to a symbol of the might of the Third Reich. Nothing, no one, must stand in the way of the Nazi will.

It's not only the humiliation of a man, the mockery of him and his religious beliefs, that catches our attention. It's also the obvious glee with which this is being done. Just look at the happy faces of the soldiers as they make sport of a man whose dignity seems to be holding up through this episode. The troops are pleased with themselves, clearly. They were possibly fortified by the motto: "The Jews are our misfortune."

Perhaps each of us might have been caught up in the aura of antiSemitism. The pressures to do so were so great that we, like so many Germans, might have succumbed to a patriotic fervor or a misguided religious zeal. During the middle 1920s, it is estimated that over 700 racist, anti-Judaic newspapers were published throughout Germany. It is in one of these, the SA organ *Sturmlied*, that these words were published: "And when Jewish blood spurts from the knife, things will go twice as well."

The men taking part in this "initiation ceremony" are all officers. While two are actively clipping locks emblematic of religious conviction, the others are apparently less interested in what is going on than in posing for the cameraman. The man second from the right certainly wants to look as handsome as he can for immortality. The tallest man went to the back of the group so as not to block out any of the others. A thoughtful person.

This, by the way, is only one of a series of photographs in which this particular Jew is the center of attraction. How long did his agony last? How long did it take to set up each of these shots? How many pictures were taken that are lost? Did the photographer promise copies of the photo to each of the officers? Did he make a good profit from the occasion? Or good contacts for future work?

Looking at massive piles of bodies of Holocaust victims may be like reading books of history about the events. The statistics are appalling but they sometimes appeal most exclusively to the intellect, which is interested in the nature of facts. Seeing individual corpses may be more like reading a novel about the Holocaust wherein our emotions are more moved.

Here we have a photograph which might evoke a variety of emotions: sorrow, horror, disgust, pity, possibly despair. We may speculate on the victim and the photographer. Perhaps both suffered in different ways. The dead man's body is emaciated. It is evident that he did not die quickly. Rather his was an extended agony. We need only to look at his hips to come to some understanding of the degree of starvation to which he was subject. Perhaps that was the cause of his death. A long look at this man's face will prove of itself a profound homily on the Holocaust.

The photographer may have undergone a certain amount of pain, too, although of a less final kind. It may have been he, out of a sense of compassion, who covered the man's penis to keep him from a kind of posthumous shame. The cameraman is clearly standing in the midst of bodies, having to be careful where he steps, perhaps fearful of tripping and falling onto the ground among the cadavers. No doubt he selected this victim as a subject because he was face up and because of that sermon on his face.

We might try to reconstruct a career, a biography, for the man shown here in the Laudsberg concentration camp, but fiction cannot approach the reality of these characters. This man was real, his pain was real and we will not intrude on that reality. Rather, let us allow him to intrude on our reality. Let us thus respond to his death rather than ignore it and thereby risk ignoring our own humanity.

In one way, the man in this photograph is fortunate. He was allowed to go to the toilet. Often prisoners in the concentration camps, while never permitted to go to the bathroom during twelve-hour work days, would not be allowed to use the facilities at night either, if the whims of the guards so dictated. We know from the work of writers like Terrence Des Pres and others that for long periods of time inmates would be covered with their own filth or that of others, given the bunk-bed arrangements in which they slept.

But while the man here is in one way lucky, his is not an enviable condition. Humiliation never is. No doubt he has seen the cameraman approach. The photograph looks like it had benefit of a flashbulb, so the prisoner knew at some point that he was being mocked. He is trying to maintain anonymity here at the trough, a trough like this in which many Jews were actually drowned because some *kapo* or guard decided that humanity would be better off that way.

Privacy of any kind was denied such prisoners. In many instances, so was paper by which men and women might clean themselves. These people, rabbis, teachers, laborers, clerks, musicians, dressmakers, remained very dirty; they smelled. Some therefore hated each other and soon hated themselves.

They were systematically degraded not only by their conquerors but also by others who were defeated by the Nazis yet who joined in league with Nazis to destroy Jews. Auschwitz, Buchenwald, Dachau, Treblinka, Sobibor, and the other infamous camps were each an entire hell thrust on people who deserved only to live lives of decency, respect, love, creativity, and whatever normalcy means.

Often a Jew walking down the street was simply picked up by the authorities and never seen by his family again. Maybe this man was just such a victim. After the disappearance of a day or so his wife and children would have to recognize that the sick feelings in their stomachs were there because the man of their family was just poof, gone. The odds were great that he would never return.

We know that in the days before very sophisticated cameras were engineered, no one could move when a shot was being taken or the film would be blurred. Hence we can deduce that this photo was "posed." The main figure in this scene was obviously forced to stand while the picture taker "got it all together." Maybe this Jew was moved around to take advantage of the right light for this shot.

But his thoughts are only tangentially on the photographer. He is miles away. Where? With a family somewhere? With an ailing brother elsewhere in the camp? With a child murdered by Nazis? With a God whose tolerance of evil puzzles him? The possibilities are enormous. Was this a face that ever laughed, told jokes, wrinkled up in playful attitude for a loved one? Did these eyes ever sparkle, show insight, compassion, understanding? Is he now vowing revenge, despairing, plotting, going mad?

This emaciated man, weighed down by a couple of bags, has the kind of look that is capable of haunting a viewer for a long time. What is in those bags, by the way? Not pistols and ammunition, not slabs of meat or packages of fresh fruit. Not cash, not a change of clothing. We will never know — but we can be sure that, as the world judges value during normal times, whatever this man was allowed to carry could not have been deemed to be of even small value. But that's irrelevant. For us, now, it's the look on his face that matters.

These bodies are tied at the feet for convenience. For convenience. Words attached to this U.S. Army documentation photograph indicate that this is a scene, a close-up of a grave, in a German camp and listed as Lager #3. The corpses are stacked five high in mass graves approximately 12 feet by 50. The victims, we read, are French, Russian, and Polish Jews who died from starvation, typhus, or poison injected by hypodermic needles. This particular pit is estimated to hold one thousand bodies. The quotation closes with an unembellished statement: "There were many such pits in the camp."

What can we think in the face of such facts? We who are used to expending our pity on "ordinary" deaths, or on those who suffer broken limbs, or on some who are beaten on the stock market, or on a friend who flunked a test, how do we express emotion over a tragedy of such magnitude? We can't be blamed, can we, for not knowing how to feel, what to feel? A certain kind of overwhelming numbness may be all that we can experience.

Tied at the feet for what? — convenience? Convenience? What mattered here was the convenience of the criminals. The victims were beneath any consideration. Often ruthless Nazis were observed showing acts of kindness to animals, indicating an apparent sincerity of attitude. How was such compassion deflected from a whole set of human beings. How is it so very many easily cooperated in Hitler's scheme of annihilation?

We cannot but be obsessed by the possibility that we too might have fallen into the moral abyss of complicity as an easy way out. Would we just follow orders as so many at war crime trials said in their defense that they did? If there is to be a final Judgment Day, do we think such an excuse will hold up before the God in whose image and likeness we are said to be created; in whose image and likeness the victims are said to have been created also?

It was German practice to photograph violence done against Jews in other countries and publish such pictures to prove how universal the hatred of Jews had become. Here is an exemplary scene with a photographer including another photographer in his record. How eager some were to try to immortalize particular events.

Note the fact that these are portable gallows, capable of being moved to various locations for the benefit of maximum attendance. Here is a way of showcasing Nazi policies, Nazi justice. And as we can see sketchily, there was a large crowd witnessing the public executions in Lodz, Poland.

The expression on the young soldier's face is far more serious, more thoughtful, than the smiles we have found on the faces of other troops who were themselves guilty of war crimes. Was this near-lad the executioner? Or is he here to guard the bodies so that the wives and children of the victims can't cut them down for decent burial? Why have the people who make up the crowd come to observe the hangings? Are they so fascinated by the event, so eager to see the instant that is universally feared? Or are these townspeople forced to witness the executions, forced to see three men made an example of?

We cannot even begin to speculate on the reasons for which these men were condemned. They may have been saboteurs, black marketeers, Jews, hostages, reprisal victims, political enemies, kin of a wanted enemy — there is no way of our telling. We do know that all of the above qualified one for the gallows. So did the stealing of food to feed one's children; so did listening to a secret radio; so did disrespectfully addressing a Nazi officer; so did . . . whim, just the whim of a Nazi could condemn a Jew or Gypsy or other foe of the Third Reich to instant death — or prolonged dying. Depending on the way a hangman ties a noose, one can die quickly or very slowly on the gallows. The executioner is, alas, one of the symbols that may be applied to this century.

In a 1950 film titled *The Gunfighter*, Gregory Peck plays a kind of sympathetic outlaw whose reputation as the "fastest gun" lures men into trying to outdraw him so that they can gain fame for shooting down the legendary figure. Early in the film, an older, obviously incompetent man, tries to kill Johnny Ringo (Peck) because the man mistakenly thinks that Ringo killed his son. When Ringo disarms the would-be avenging father and claims innocence of the boy's murder, the unbelieving elderly cowboy says that Ringo probably has forgotten the incident. Ringo responds with words something like this: "You never forget a man you kill."

That seems like such a truism. But mass destruction of human beings shows how empty such a statement can be. Nowhere is this more true than in the Nazi atrocities. It is very likely, given what we know of the attempted annihilation of the Jews, that all of the bodies pictured in this photograph from Latvia fell before one executioner. Surely this man, like the many multiple murderers of World War II, did not remember all of his victims.

To him, these were not men and women and children; these were vermin, individual pestilences. He knew them no more than we know termites or water bugs that we try to stamp out in large numbers.

Generally, even when we do exterminate such pests, we do not do so in such large quantities as did the Nazi destroyers and their collaborators. The numbers of bodies in this, as in so many photographic documents that exist, are uncountable. Piled on top of each other so randomly and quantitatively they are like a tiny Milky Way when seen through a telescope — so undistinguishable because so disorderly and great in number. What we see here is not even an hour's "work," and the soldiers worked very long hours we know.

Several days after liberation of the Nazi SS murder camp at Ohrdruf in Germany, the accompanying scene took place. The supreme commander-in-chief of the Allied armies, General Dwight Eisenhower, viewed the charred remains of some of the victims. With him were Generals Omar Bradley and George Patton, Jr. Eyewitnesses said that between three and four thousand prisoners were slain here, seventy just before the American troops arrived. These were from Czechoslovakia, the Soviet Union, Belgium and France.

The experience so moved Eisenhower that he wrote a letter to Chief-of-Staff George Marshall in which he said that "the things I saw beggar description.... The visual evidence and the verbal testimony of starvation, cruelty, and bestiality were so overpowering as to leave me a bit sick. In one room, where there were piled up twenty or thirty naked men, killed by starvation, George Patton would not even enter. He said he would get sick if he did so. I made the visit deliberately, in order to be in a position to give *first-hand* evidence of these things if ever, in the future, there develops a tendency to charge these allegations merely to 'propaganda.' "

However we define hope, we see here a man who has none. His anguish is not superficial; it has penetrated his soul. To speculate on the cause of this victim's condition might be to dishonor him. But we may wonder if he survived the moment. His pain seems too complete, so overwhelming that this may have been the final expression of his life.

Jewish psychiatrists who themselves had concentration camp experiences have written about how some (of the few) who survived the death camps were able to do so. Bruno Bettelheim suggests that certain men and women took on the personality of their aggressors in order to get through alive. Leo Eitinger, after having analyzed many patients who, like himself, barely outlived Auschwitz and other camps, feels that one almost indispensable element to the survival of many was having a close relative sharing the atrocity experiences. Those who lost their entire families or who were separated from them in a kind of absolute way did not have this opportunity. Viktor Frankl, the founder of logotherapy, a psychiatric approach based on hope — the hope of being reunited with a loved one, of completing a particular project — saw such hope as being important to a relatively large number of survivors.

But the man in this photograph seems to have none of these. His posture is of one hardly aggressive in any form. Furthermore, here he seems so alone that abandonment by family, friends, even God, appears to be reflected in his cry. And it is despair, not hope, that is reflected in his face, a despair that may have come from a realization that he is a creature suspended on earth, with ties to no one, no thing.

Nor are we taking into account any physical pain this person is suffering. How cold is he? How long has it been since he has eaten? Is disease ravaging his body the way it did nearly all who lived for any length of time in the death camps? In a culture saturated with the false emotions of Hollywood, television soap operas, advertisers, self-pitiers, and sycophants in general, can we long contemplate the true emotion of this miserable, miserable human being? We must.

Chapter 4

Toward Reconciliation

In 1944, as the Second World War was nearing its end, a papal nuncio is reported to have said this: "There is no innocent blood of Jewish children in the world. All Jewish blood is guilty. You have to die. This is the punishment that has been awaiting you because of [deicide]."[1]

To a survivor of the Holocaust, the perspective is quite different. Alexander Donat in *The Holocaust Kingdom* says that this question was raised in the death camp: "How can Christianity survive the discovery that after a thousand years of its being Europe's official religion, Europe remains pagan at heart?"[2]

Contemporary literature, the great barometer of the pressures of the subconscious, raises that question in perhaps an even more fundamental way. What is reality? We need only to read the novels of Alain Robbe-Grillet, Nathalie Sarraute, Carlos Fuentes, Gabriel García Márquez, Raymond Queneau, Kurt Vonnegut, Samuel Beckett, Severo Sarduy, and many others, from nations that have been identified as Christian, to know that the questions about the meaning of existence are being asked again because the pre-Auschwitz and pre-Buchenwald pat answers we had went up in the flames of ovens that were prepared for Jews and others.

Questioning, of course, is an absolute necessity today. As a friend told the young Elie Wiesel, just before Wiesel was to be shipped to a death camp: "I pray to the God within me that He

---

[1] Quoted by Irving Greenberg in "Judaism and Christianity after the Holocaust," in *Journal of Ecumenical Studies* 12 (Fall 1975), p. 526.

[2] New York, 1965, pp. 230–231.

will give me the strength to ask Him the right questions."[3] Novelists and philosophers known as the Absurdists ask questions from
despair. This seems appropriate for those in the class of persecutors. What is amazing is that the victims — the Jews — are mainly
able to ask their questions in a framework of hope.

However, the hope has its roots in experience and is not a naive,
childish desire. I heard someone ask Wiesel if he believed in God.
His reply should be made known to all Christians. "If I told you
that I believe in God, I would be lying; if I told you that I did not
believe in God, I would be lying. If I told you that I believe in man,
I would be lying; if I told you I did not believe in man, I would be
lying. But one thing I do know: the Messiah has not come yet." In
The Crucifixion of the Jews, Protestant theologian Franklin H. Littell
has written, from his Christian perspective:

> The truth about the murder of European Jewry by baptized Christians is
> this: it raises in a most fundamental way the question of the credibility
> of Christianity. Was Jesus a false messiah? No one can be a true messiah
> whose followers feel compelled to torture and destroy other human
> persons who think differently. Is the Jewish people, after all and in
> spite of two millennia of Christian calumny, the true Suffering Servant
> promised in Isaiah? (p. 16)

Littell has observed, it was noted earlier, that if Christ and Peter and
Paul had lived during the Nazi period, they would have perished
at Auschwitz. We may be forgiven for asking if maybe they did.
Perhaps these deaths were, in a sense preparatory to a resurrection
in a meaningful, spiritual sense. Christianity, as an ideal, has been
less than inspiringly visible. The Christianity of the Cross may
have been present, in a large part, only ironically in history. J.
Coert Rylarsdaam saw that if being a Christian meant the taking
up of the Cross and being crucified for God, then the only practicing
Christians are the Jews![4] Russian thinker Nicolas Berdyaev would
have agreed: "Perhaps the saddest thing to admit is that those who
rejected the Cross have to carry it, while those who welcomed it
are as often engaged in crucifying others."[5]

It is clear that we Christians may not hide behind the hero-

---

[3]*Night*, p. 16.
[4]Cf. *Journal of Ecumenical Studies* 12 (Fall 1975), p. 541.
[5]*Christianity and Anti-Semitism* (Kent, 1952), p. 12.

ics of Franz Jagersdatter, Alfred Delp, Dietrich Bonhoeffer and the
relatively few others who identified evil as evil, refused to rationalize or compromise with it, and died as martyrs in Hitler's time.
We may not take for granted that we would have been numbered
with them had the opportunity arisen. If Original Sin includes us,
so does Auschwitz. In retaining the Bible while denying the people who are its subject, we Christians are guilty of arrogance. In
declaring ourselves the people of the New Israel, we are guilty of
arrogance.

A serious ecumenism must be attempted, on a level far higher
than what we are experiencing currently. I've personally lived in
over a dozen dioceses since the end of the war against the Jews
and I've travelled extensively throughout the nation and I have
noticed only modest ecumenical efforts on the part of official Chris-
tendom — yet Auschwitz requires extraordinary ecumenical effort.
Most of what I can see is similar to a Russian Five Year Farm Plan.
The right offices are established, the right papers are filled out with
comforting figures, but at the end of the period, where is the grain?

Let me offer a series of points that I feel we, as Christians, might
implement in order to bring us closer to our Jewish brothers and
sisters, people we have violently alienated for so long. Basically,
the suggestions are aimed at institutional actions rather than individual. This is intentional, because it would be presumptuous for
one Christian to tell another how to best react to history. That will
have to be a personal approach. But because we are all a part of the
church, it is not only appropriate but imperative that we require of
the church certain acts in our name. It will take experts in various
disciplines to more fully elaborate on each of the points below, but
let me merely list them, then comment briefly on each:

1. The Catholic church should excommunicate Adolf Hitler.

2. The Christian liturgical calendar(s) should include an annual
    memorial service for Jewish victims of the Holocaust.

3. We Christians must publicly and officially admit the errors of
    our teachers where they were wrong concerning Jews.

4. The Christian churches must insist on the essential Jewish-
    ness of Christianity.

5. Jesus should be recognized as a link between Jews and Christians.

6. The churches' teaching on the subject of evil needs to be reevaluated.

7. Traditional Christian theologies of history must be reexamined.

8. The Vatican historical archives for the twentieth century need to be opened to historians.

9. Chairs of Judaic studies ought to be established at more Christian colleges and universities.

10. Christian schools should adopt Holocaust curricula as integral segments of their overall instructional plans.

11. Christian seminaries should teach future ministers the history and theological implications of anti-Judaism in general and of the Holocaust specifically.

12. We might look to see if a redefinition of the notion of inspiration in Christian Scripture is appropriate.

13. Christians must find new terminology for what we now designate as the Old Testament and the New Testament.

14. Catholics must demand an encyclical letter that deals specifically with the sins of anti-Judaism and with the sins of Christians in their actions toward Jews.

15. The heavy Christian emphasis on missionizing should be redirected toward perfecting individual lives.

16. We Christians need to get on our knees and repent our sins against Jewish people.

Undoubtedly this list should be considerably larger and readers may wish to adds points for consideration. However, these sixteen, important as I see them, are offered for starters at least. Each deserves some elaboration.

1. *The Catholic church should excommunicate Adolf Hitler.*

Excommunication is, we know, a punishment meted out by the official church to living persons whose conduct is considered to be scandalous from a Christian moral viewpoint. Hence there has been no purpose, traditionally, for imposing such a penalty on a dead person. But I think that we need to show our Jewish friends that with this belated act we are serious about developing ecumenical interaction with Jews. Hitler died with his name still on the tax rolls of the Catholic church. Jews know that and find the fact incredible. So do Christians who are made aware. It is true that the top Nazi was not a practicing Catholic but his symbolic, public position requires that he should have been publicly disavowed. Women and men have been denied participation in the church's sacraments for *comparatively* trivial acts: divorce and remarriage, stealing papal property, dueling, voting for the communist party in Italy — it has recently even been threatened against certain priests who have persisted in saying the mass in Latin. But Hitler somehow did not qualify! Posthumous excommunication would not only be an ecumenical sign, it would also show today's neo-Nazis that their anti-Jewish activities will not be tolerated by the Catholic church.

2. *The Christian liturgical calendar(s) should include an annual memorial service for Jewish victims of the Holocaust.*

This will not only indicate to the Jewish community that a new spirit is emerging, it will also help to energize Christian consciences about the awe-ful event. Germany's Catholic novelist Günter Grass has written that "what is asked of us is to understand Auschwitz in its historical past, recognize it in the present and not assume blindly that Auschwitz lies behind us."[6] I suggest that one important way to remember the Holocaust in all of its significance is through liturgical memorialization on a regular basis. Preachers would be thus encouraged to discuss its implications and congregations would be awakened to them.

3. *We as Christians must publicly and officially admit the errors of our teachers where they were wrong concerning Jews.*

This will be a long, ongoing process. It would be ludicrous, after over 1500 years of calumny toward Jews (or at best of official silence where holy words were necessary), to say simply we're sorry and to expect the scales thus to be balanced. Certain statements of St. John

---

[6]Quoted in Eva Fleischner, *Judaism in German Christian Theology since 1945* (Metuchen, N.J., 1975), p. 21.

Chrysostom and St. Justin and St. Cyprian and St. Hippolytus and St. Bernard of Clairvaux and the all-star list of anti-Judaists must be contradicted so that the world will know that we abjure these words. It is not enough that this theologian or that writer or a particular bishop say the necessary things. But officially, popes and patriarchs and bishops' councils and pastors in the pulpit, in their parish bulletins, in the diocesan newspapers, and everywhere else appropriate begin and continue to teach the love of Jews.

4. *The Christian churches must insist on the essential Jewishness of Christianity.*

This point will need elaboration only for the theologically retarded. And yet it is necessary for us to consider the harm that anti-Judaism does to Christians at the same time that we discuss the victimization of Jews. Every antiSemite is a slave — a slave to hatred of a particular kind. Dr. Martin Luther King, Jr., seriously cared about the effect of racism on the racist. He knew that the psychological danger to the person who hates may, in the longer view, be far more disastrous to *that* person's group, to the persecutor's group, than to the people being tormented. What has happened to the Christian psyche over the centuries? How have we withstood the boomerang assault of antiSemitism? How can we square St. Paul's teaching on the greatness of charity while supporting — at least by our silence — exile, ghettoization, imprisonment, torture, and murder of Jews?

5. *Jesus should be recognized as a link between Jews and Christians.*

This point is a logical derivative of the previous one, on the essential Jewishness of Christianity. Too often Jesus has been offered as a stumbling block between Christians and Jews, as a rationale for mutual exclusion. Here is an excerpt from a document written under the sponsorship of the Commission on Faith and Order of the National Council of Churches and the Secretariat for Catholic-Jewish Relations of the National Conference of Catholic Bishops:

> The Church of Christ is rooted in the life of the People of Israel. We Christians look upon Abraham as our spiritual ancestor and father of our faith.... The ministry of Jesus and the life of the early Christian community were thoroughly rooted in the Judaism of their day, par-

ticularly in the teachings of the Pharisees. The Christian Church is
still sustained by the living faith of the patriarchs and prophets, kings
and priests, scribes and rabbis, and the people whom God chose for his
own. Christ is the link . . . enabling the Gentiles to be numbered among
Abraham's 'offspring' and therefore fellow-heirs with the Jews according to God's promise. It is a tragedy of history that Jesus, our bond of
unity with the Jews, has all too often become a symbol and source of
division and bitterness because of human weakness and pride.[7]

Tragedy of history indeed — for Jews, for Christians.

   6. *The churches' teachings on the subject of evil need to be reevaluated.*
   St. Thomas Aquinas has carried the burden of traditional thinking on this subject. He identified evil as nothing, no-thing, an
absence of a good or perfection. (We are here basically speaking
of moral evil, which is equated with sin, rather than physical evil,
e.g., damage wrought by such natural phenomena as earthquakes,
or metaphysical evil, which is attributed to limitations due to the
finiteness of the human condition.) Carl Gustav Jung has written
convincingly on the psychological need for each of us as individuals, and for collective groups such as nations, to recognize the
role of evil in our natures and in our actions. Consideration of the
deaths of the nearly six million Jews, and the deaths of the fifty
million in World War II, force us to inquire further as to the nature
of evil. It is possible that a key to a fuller understanding on this
topic will be found in the movement popularly designated as process theology. To caricaturize the teachings in process theology we
might say that it applies certain principles of evolution to God's development. God is not static, God changes, and part of that change
is determined by our activities. If this is true, perhaps the same is
true of Satan as well. At any rate, the possibilities for insight from
process thought seem very great and ought to be studied.

   7. *Traditional Christian theologies of history need to be reexamined.*
   Generally, history has been regarded as the unfolding plan of
God for humanity, or as a *Weltanschauung* based on the providen-
tial action of God in human affairs. For many today, it is difficult

---

[7]Michael B. McGarry, *Christology after Auschwitz* (New York, 1977), pp. 57–58.

to see how the Holocaust fits into such concepts. Karl Rahner, one of the most influential Christian thinkers of our era, says that many questions regarding the theology of history require considerable study. Among those he indicates are the purposive unity of human history, the theology of history before Christ, the sanctification of the entire sphere of the "profane" through the Christian church and much more, including the very basic problem of the theological meaning of a theology of history. Those of us who are nearly overwhelmed by Auschwitz feel a terrible inability to put its relevance into any pattern. Many feel it is outside of any overall plan. If true, that must be reflected in our analysis of the meaning of history.

8. *The Vatican historical archives for the twentieth century need to be opened to historians.*

There are two aspects to this suggestion; one might be termed positive, the other negative. We might ask, what is the value gained by having Vatican documents unavailable to the scholars? Are events of that period so shameful to the Catholic church that they need to be hidden? That is certainly one conclusion being drawn by some people. It isn't enough for Vatican officials to make responses to criticism of church action and inaction during and just preceding the Nazi period. Such responses are of the "if you only had all the facts, you'd see things in a more favorable light" variety. Well then, give us the facts. If Pius XII's reputation is being besmirched because of ignorance based only on speculation, let us have the rest of the story.

Rolf Hochhuth's drama *The Deputy* was scorned by certain churchmen in its emphasis on Pius XII's inaction regarding the persecution of Jews. But the suspicions of the rest of us who "don't have the full picture" are not put to rest merely because some bishops say that they should be. What has Rome to hide? If little or nothing, we should know that so that the prestige of the papacy may be considerably restored. If there are, in fact, as many believe, monumental errors of judgment (to put it one way), which the archives will reveal, we must know that also. *All* of the facts need to be revealed. If it is found that the hierarchy of the church, in a sense acting for many of us, behaved immorally, that must be revealed and admissions must be made and, yes, penance must be begun. How can we correct past abuses unless we know them?

Indeed we may be condemned to repeat these errors, as George Santayana would suggest, unless we recognize them as such. But we cannot know them fully if the Vatican, claiming a purpose of promulgating truth, in fact hides the truth.

A second aspect of what some see as a Vatican coverup, what might be described as a silence after the Silence, is the right of certain persons to their good names. There are, we know, a number of Christians, relatively small yet not insignificant, who aided Jews during the decade 1935–1945. And some did so with great personal risk. There were those who lost their lives in this holy work. Their actions need to be made public not only for their sakes, but for ours as well. The rest of us are starving for stories of Christian heroes during this period. We are depressed, psychologically battered, by the contrary evidence. Our emotional balance requires more than what we have now in the knowledge of Christians actively being Christian on behalf of Jews. Undoubtedly there is evidence for this in the Vatican archives. Why is this, too, being suppressed?

9. *Chairs of Judaic studies ought to be established at more Christian colleges and universities.*

This has been done at a few institutions around the world, but if we are to make a serious effort at learning about Judaism — and in an important sense therefore learning about our Christian heritage — such chairs of study are well advised. Furthermore, they ought properly to be funded by Christian groups rather than Jewish ones. Again, we need to let the world in general, and Jewish women and men in particular, know that we Christians are serious in our attempts at coming closer to Jews in a very true spiritual way. And perhaps it need not be said, yet perhaps it does, that Jewish as well as Christian scholars be appointed to such posts.

In one of the recent crises of growth in the United States, few recommended that black studies programs be exclusively taught and directed by white teachers and administrators on campus. Men were not being asked to develop women's academic programs. The analogy is obvious and, ultimately, does warrant mention since for so long, at so many schools, Jewish Scripture and tradition were taught exclusively by non-Jews. Perhaps there will come a time when such an arrangement will be more acceptable — both when Christians have become radically immersed in their pre-Jesus roots and when the pains of persecutions of Jews are of historical memory only — but this is not such a time, nor can we see it in the near or, alas, even the reasonably remote future.

10. *Christian schools should adopt Holocaust curricula as integral segments of their overall instructional plans.*

An increasing number of public school systems are doing so; the specifically Christian institutions need to as well. The role that Christianity has had in the persecution of Jews needs to be introduced to students by trained teachers who can meet the challenges that such courses will necessarily prove to be. However, ignoring the issue is to fail the pursuit of truth and no Christian, we would hope no human being, would be averse to that pursuit. "Trained teachers" implies a program for the instructors as well, and more and more of this kind of help is becoming available, particularly through Holocaust centers around the nation.

11. *Christian seminaries should teach future ministers the history and theological implications of anti-Judaism in general and the Holocaust specifically.*

Many priests and Protestant ministers are shockingly ignorant in this area. Some drastic overhauling is necessary if this dangerous, yes dangerous, situation is to be corrected. How is it possible that men and women, ordained to be channels of God's grace, are unaware where their own tradition has been blockage to transmission? This is one of the most serious problems facing a corrective to ignorance of the Holocaust and its antecedents. The ministers are preachers to the faithful. How are they to teach what they do not know?

12. *We might look to see if a redefinition of the notion of inspiration in Christian Scripture is appropriate.*

Gregory Baum wrote this as a priest: "If the Church wants to clear itself of the anti-Jewish trends built into its teaching, a few marginal correctives will not do. It must examine the very center of its proclamation and reinterpret the meaning of the gospel for our times."[8] He presses further and insists that "what the encounter of Auschwitz demands of Christian theologians, therefore, is that

---

[8]In his introduction to Rosemary Radford Ruether, *Faith and Fratricide* (New York, 1974), pp. 6–7.

they submit Christian teaching to a radical ideological critique."[9] Some Christian theologians admit of no anti-Jewish bias in their Bible, but that seems indefensible today. Others see this bias but maintain that this comes not from inspiration, but by interpolation of early Christians to meet certain contemporary exegeses. An eloquent current voice on this subject is Rosemary Radford Ruether, whose book *Faith and Fratricide* has caused many to ask for a more complete exploration of Christian teachings on biblical inspiration. To quote Baum once again, " . . . what if God is addressing that Church anew through the awful event of the holocaust?"[10] Ruether and others are asking the same question. We can ignore it on no level, including the level of Scripture study.

13. *Christians must find new terminology for what we now designate as the Old Testament and the New Testament.*

Most Christians do not seem to be aware of how insulting these titles can be to Jews. At the very least, we can be seen as arrogant in implying by these names that "we" have appropriated "their" Book, updated it, fulfilled it, and somehow have cornered the market on interpreting that earlier body of work. Indeed many, many Christian theologians, when teaching Genesis, Leviticus, Isaiah, never even consult Jewish commentators regarding exegeses of these works. In writing about pre-Christian biblical texts, Fr. John Pawlikowski, who is in the department of historical and doctrinal studies at Catholic Theological Union in Chicago, had this to say in *The National Catholic Reporter* (April 21, 1978):

> At best we see them as a prelude to the fullness of teaching found in the New Testament, not as containing religious insights vital in their own right. At worst, the term [Old Testament] allows the church to totally ignore the rich spirituality found in these writings and to continue to parrot the totally discredited notion of Christianity as the religion of love in contrast to Judaism's dependence on legalism.

Later Pawlikowski suggests that the term "New Testament" might be replaced by the designation "Apostolic writings," originally offered by Dr. Eugene Fisher, director of the National Conference of Catholic Bishops' Secretariat for Catholic-Jewish Relations.

---

[9]Ibid., p. 7.
[10]Ibid., p. 8.

The term "Hebrew Scriptures," Pawlikowski notes further, "forces upon us a recognition of Judaism as a separate religious tradition whose Scriptures we share but do not own." There are problems here, including the fact that the pre-Christian Scriptures for Roman Catholics include certain Greek works that are not a part of the Hebrew canon, and I am not insisting on any particular new name for what is now referred to as the Old Testament. But I am urging a change of title that Jews will find acceptable and that will be, in an important sense, truer.

14. *Catholics must demand an encyclical letter that deals specifically with the sins of antiSemitism and with the sins of Christians in their actions toward Jews.*

In the second chapter of this book, a written but unpublished encyclical on this subject was briefly discussed. Pope Pius XI had commissioned such a letter but died (under suspicious circumstances), and it is believed by many that the publication of the encyclical would have had an important effect on the prosecution of the program of annihilation of the Jews that was implemented so forcefully not long after Pius XI's death. It is well known that when Christianity, speaking through certain church officials, objected to the implementation of Hitler's euthanasia plan (which was to put to death "unproductive" citizens — the aged, the retarded, the terminally ill, for example) the Germans quickly reacted by officially abandoning the practice. It is not too much to believe that a strong reaction by Rome to anti-Judaism as it was raging at the time would have had important consequences for all humanity.

Pius XI's document concluded by urging all of the world's Catholic clergy to work against antiSemitism (and racism) everywhere. In the unpublished letter we read that no totalitarian government by its nature can understand the concept of the common good. It can be observed that in such governments, "no hesitation is felt at simply stripping men of their liberty and still less hesitation at violating the sanctity of house and home." We read later that "the very essence of the State [is] to recognize in all men an equal right to life; a recognition which cannot be avoided and a right to be protected by law." And then the document becomes hard hitting: "The theory and practice of racism which makes a distinction between the higher and lower races ignores the bond of unity.... " And later, and more specifically (for our purposes), the letter makes reference to the Nuremberg Laws, whose bases were totally anti-Judaic: "What a fearful insult to a race and what a degradation of humanity when marriage between the members of different racial groups is systematically prohibited. . . . It is further increased when it becomes clear that the struggle for racial purity ends by becoming uniquely the struggle against the Jews." And for a final passage from this much needed work: In response to anti-Judaism, "the answer of the church is unequivocal and unchanging. Her answer is determined by no earthly policy, but by her fidelity to the truth bequeathed to her custody by her Divine Founder. . . . It established a universal Kingdom, in which there would be no distinction of Jew or Gentile, Greek or barbarian. . . . These same doctrines likewise show the utter unfitness and inefficacy of anti-Semitism." As Michael Mashberg, writing in the *National Jewish Monthly* (April 1978), p. 46, has judged: "If the Vatican chooses not to publish [this encyclical] as an historical document and make known the circumstances surrounding Pius XII's attitude toward the encyclical, then, the silence of the Vatican will increase the din of its critics and magnify Pope Pius XII's refusal to issue a condemnation of Nazi racial policies." In an important way, Christians too have been failed by the nonpublication of the treatise. We must demand that it be made public, or a letter expressly like it, and that it be given official church endorsement.

15. *The heavy Christian emphasis on missionizing should be redirected toward perfecting individual Christian lives.*

Missionary efforts, however well intentioned, are generally not as well received by the presumed beneficiaries as they are enthusiastically endorsed by those of the performing group. Perhaps Christians might comprehend this better if they tried to imagine how they would react if Jews tried to convert us to Judaism. The true missionary activity, we must realize, is in the perfection of our individual, personal lives. If what we do, if how we live, is worthy of emulation, that will be missionary activity enough.

An example in the right direction may be seen in the work of the Congregation of Notre Dame de Sion, founded in France in 1846. This religious order was begun by two brothers, Marie Alphonse and Marie Theodore Ratisbonne, Catholic converts from Judaism, with avowed aims to bring about a better understanding between Christians and Jews and for the conversion of the latter. Now, however, the women and men who are followers of the Ratisbonnes (the men's group is called the Fathers of Sion) insist that prose-lytizing must be completely abandoned, and they are leaders in efforts in Christian-Jewish dialogue.

16. *We Christians need to get on our knees and repent our sins against the Jewish people.*

I mean the Jews of history: past, present, yes, future Jews too. They must all understand that we know of our errors and that we have a collective (and individual) firm purpose of amendment. One way to prove this, of course, will be, when we get off our knees, to work for some of the suggestions made above, and for other ideas that will be developed by informed persons. However, as we approach our Jewish friends with suggestions, with plans, and in dialogue, we must do so in the spirit that Irving Green-berg demands of us: "Let us offer this fundamental criterion after the Holocaust. No statement, theological or otherwise, should be made that would not be credible in the presence of burning children."[11]

---

[11] In Eva Fleischner, ed., *Auschwitz: Beginning of a New Era?* (New York, 1977), p. 23.

Afterword

Like Harry James Cargas, I am a Catholic, born in America, too young to have served in World War II, fortunate enough to recall the events of forty years ago only as history, impersonally, my family spared the carnage that consumed so many lives.

And like Harry, I find it necessary to remember. As a Christian, I know I can't afford the price of silence, to ignore the record of what was done, to turn away from an evil so immense and overwhelming that it can frighten us into mute acceptance.

So I am grateful to Harry for this appeal to the Christian conscience — and the world conscience.

He affirms our need, now more than ever, to insist that everyone remember the millions who suffered, the millions who were murdered. Why now? First, because — as impossible as it seems, as incredible to believe in view of what we know — antiSemitism still lives.

Despite the horror of the box cars and the gas chambers and the crematoria, despite the careful records the Nazis kept, there are those who deny that the Holocaust ever happened. They still preach their ancient lies. They invent new reasons to justify their venom. They invite us to deny what is so difficult to comprehend, the true purpose of antiSemitism, the end to which it led.

But as dangerous and persistent as these people are, they are not the only reason why we must speak out loudly, why we must keep before the world the true record of what happened. The truth is, even those who are free of antiSemitism — even those who are almost certainly sincere in their revulsion at the Holocaust — are tempted to forget, to declare this ugly chapter of human history closed, done with, over. This temptation is understandable and, therefore, all the more dangerous.

For to confront the fact of the Holocaust is to look into the heart of darkness, to comprehend the scope of evil in this world, to measure the human capacity to hate and to murder and to destroy. It is to acknowledge the abyss. And the world resists doing so.

Amid the piles of nuclear armaments — amid the wars that wrack our planet, amid the homelessness, the epidemics, the famine — it becomes harder and harder to deal with the Holocaust, to face the reality it represents for the entire human race. But the harder it becomes, the more necessary it becomes. The more necessary it is that we have people like Harry James Cargas to keep us focused. None of us can afford to deny or to forget, to lose that focus, to be silent.

We all must look — Gentiles as much as Jews. We all must understand — Americans as well as Europeans. We all must preserve and honor the memory of those who died. This all of us must do, not out of hatred or revenge or rancor. But out of love. Out of love for our brothers and sisters crowded into death camps, starved and beaten and degraded, shot and gassed . . . and incinerated. Out of love for ourselves, for our children, for the future we must share.

Harry James Cargas recognized this imperative decades ago. He dedicated himself to struggling against the silence that made the Holocaust possible, to insisting that such passivity never be repeated. He speaks in this book for those who died. For those who survived. For those still voiceless and oppressed. For the generations yet to come. His message is one we must all take to heart: in the name of God and humanity, "never again."

MARIO CUOMO
Governor of New York

Bibliography

Following is a suggested approach to further reading on the Holocaust. Hundreds of important books are available in English and those listed below are only a part of them, but these are among the best.

The most comprehensive single-volume history of the Holocaust is Raul Hilberg's *The Destruction of the European Jews* (3 vols., New York: Holmes and Meier, 1973) while the most readable may be *The Holocaust* by Nora Levin (New York: Schocken, 1973).

Background reading for the rise of Nazi antiSemitism is important to understanding how Hitler's policies were so readily accepted. *The Anguish of the Jews* (New York: Paulist, 1985) is an excellent survey of Christian antiSemitism by a Catholic priest, Edward Flannery. Peter Viereck traces the development of Nazi ideology in *Meta-politics* (New York: Capricorn, 1961) subtitled, "The Roots of the Nazi Mind."

Biographies and memoirs of the most influential of the Nazis are helpful for understanding their appeal. Hitler's *Mein Kampf* (New York: Houghton Mifflin, 1943) was the bible of his movement, spelling out clearly what his destructive ideas were. Rudolf Hoess's *Commandant at Auschwitz* (New York: World, 1961) is the confession of the man executed for his role in heading the most notorious of the death camps. Other titles in this category are *Albert Speer* by Matthias Schmidt (New York: St. Martin, 1984), about the minister of armaments and war production for the Third Reich. Tom Bower's *Klaus Barbie* (New York, 1984) details the atrocities of a Gestapo chief in France. The life of the Nazi minister of propaganda is rendered in *Goebbels* by Helmut Heiber (New York: Quality, 1983). A collection of shorter chapters on Nazi individuals is found in Joachim Fest's *The Face of the Third Reich* (New York: Pantheon, 1977).

Memoirs of victims are among the most powerful Holocaust books. Elie Wiesel's *Night* (New York: Bantam, 1982) is a classic in its field. In *The Death Brigade* (New York: Schocken, 1978) Leon Wells tells of his being forced, as a prisoner, to obliterate traces of Nazi massacres. Charlotte Delbo's *None of Us Will Return* (Boston: Beacon, 1978) is an angry, moving document about life and death in a women's camp. Alexander Donat's *The Holocaust Kingdom* (New York: Schocken, 1978) provides extensive details of life in the Warsaw Ghetto and in labor and death camps. For good reason, Primo Levi's *Survival in Auschwitz* (New York: Macmillan, 1961) remains one of the best known of the Holocaust memoirs. Andre Stein's probing confrontation with his own past — *Broken Silence* (Toronto, 1984) — is beautifully written.

There are various approaches that authors have taken to reflect on the Shoa. Eva Fleischner edited a volume of addresses in *Auschwitz: Beginning of a New Era?* (New York: Ktav, 1978) in which important thinkers discuss the Holocaust and antiSemitism. *Harry James Cargas in Conversation with Elie Wiesel* (New York: Paulist, 1976) is the record of three days of dialogue between a Catholic and a Jewish survivor who was to win the Nobel Peace Prize; the conversation is about the Holocaust and about Wiesel himself. Another Jewish-Christian cooperative effort is *Approaches to Auschwitz* by Richard Rubenstein and John Roth (Atlanta, 1987), an excellent approach to the Holocaust and its legacy. Terrence Des Pres renders an anatomy of life in the death camps in *The Survivor* (New York: Oxford, 1976) and Simon Wiesenthal, the Nazi hunter, discusses with others the issue of forgiveness of Nazis for their crimes in *The Sunflower* (New York: Schocken, 1976).

A particularly Christian perspective is offered by Franklin Littell in *The Crucifixion of the Jews* (New York: Harper & Row, 1975). Abraham Peck has brought together seven intelligent essays in *Jews and Christians after the Holocaust* (Philadelphia, 1982) and Anna Pawelczynska gives a Polish sociologists perspective in *Values and Violence in Auschwitz* (Berkeley: University of California Press, 1979). An angry Jewish response to religious implications is Eliezer Berkovit's *Faith after the Holocaust* (New York: Ktav, 1973).

Good fiction about a subject can frequently have a greater impact on readers than straight history has. There have been some very weak efforts of writing about the Holocaust, but some outstanding ones as well. Among these latter are Andre Schwarz-

Bart's *The Last of the Just* (New York: Bantam, 1961), Piotr Rawicz's *Blood from the Sky* (New York: Harcourt, Brace, and World, 1963), Meritt Linn's *A Book of Songs* (New York: New American Library, 1983), and a series of works by Arnost Lustig, especially *Darkness Casts No Shadows* (Evanston: Northwestern University Press, 1976), *Night and Hope* (New York: Avon, 1985), and *The Unloved* (New York, 1985). Tadeusz Borowski provides stunning short stories in *This Way for the Gas, Ladies and Gentlemen* (New York: Viking, 1967).

For a more complete guide to reading see my second edition of *The Holocaust: An Annotated Bibliography* (Chicago: Catholic Library Association, 1985) in which 425 books are described in 150–200 words each.

Index